Honorée Corder

Author, *The Successful Single Mom* book series

IF DIVORCE IS A GAME, THESE ARE THE RULES

8 Rules for Thriving Before, During and After Divorce

Published by Honorée Enterprises Publishing, LLC.

Copyright 2014
©Honorée Enterprises Publishing, LLC & Honorée Corder

ISBN: 978-0-9916696-9-1

Discover other titles by Honorée Corder at
http://www.HonoreeCorder.com, Amazon.com,
BarnesandNoble.com, Smashwords.com and on iBooks.

Additional titles by Honorée Corder

Paying4College: How to Save 25-50% on Your Child's College Education (with Beth Walker)

Play2Pay: How to Market Your College-Bound Student-Athlete for Scholarship Money (with Beth Walker)

Tall Order! 7 Master Strategies to Organize Your Life and Double Your Success in Half the Time

The Successful Single Dad

The Successful Single Mom Cooks! Cookbook

The Successful Single Mom Finds Love

The Successful Single Mom Gets Fit!

The Successful Single Mom Gets Rich!

The Successful Single Mom: Get Your Life Back and Your Game On!

Madre Soltera y Exitosa {Spanish version}

Vision to Reality: How Short Term Massive Action Equals Long Term Maximum Results

Table of Contents

Dear Reader,

Welcome to *If Divorce is a Game, These are the Rules*. I wrote this book because my own divorce had such a profound effect on me, and in many ways still does. I had a really hard time, and felt alone as though I was the only person in the world going through it. As a former military wife and single mom, I felt I was an outcast in some ways, and incredibly ill-equipped to handle the situation, and my new life, on my own. I could find no guidebook -- or rule-book -- to help me navigate not only the divorce, but finding my "sea legs" after the divorce, *and* one that would help me to intentionally release the divorce, and design and create a new life.

This book comes on the heels of the success of *The Successful Single Mom* book series. I wrote the first book in the series as I was getting re-married and enjoying the fruits of my personal and professional development. But not all of my readers are moms, or even women, and they have let me know there is a gap that needed to be filled. This book is meant to close that gap for anyone who is dealing with, or has dealt with, their own divorce ... and wants to get on with gettin' on!

I meet far too many people who are holding a grudge against their exes. They are stuck in "divorce mud," unable to move forward because they either don't know that they can, don't know how to, or both.

I know for sure with a reference guide I would have done a better job of getting a divorce, been a better ex-wife sooner, a better co-parent, and I for sure would have had the tools and strategies to create a life I love *much much sooner.*

This book makes the assumption that you are in the process of a divorce, or, although your divorce has been finalized, it is still fresh in your mind. It speaks to the person who knows there is absolutely no way their marriage could be saved, and they are fully – okay, at least partially -- open to the possibility that their divorce, while at times miserable and painful, could just be one of the best things that has ever happened to them.

If Divorce is a Game is just such a guidebook, written for you to help you come into your own after your divorce, with as much grace and ease as possible, and in a shorter period of time than going it alone.

Are you ready? Let's go!

To your best success!

Honorée Corder
Visionary, Strategist, Writer, Coach, Wife, Mom

PROLOGUE

Who am I?

I'm a writer, executive coach, business coach, speaker, friend, wife (and ex-wife), mom, and above all, an optimist.

I'm also a divorced woman with ten years of "being divorced" experience, and experience in working with, talking to, and helping men and women (and sometimes their children) as they attempt to traverse their divorce journey.

I've seen and heard almost everything. *I cheated. She cheated. He's a drug addict. I'm a workaholic. She chose her tennis coach. He never got off the couch.* The story doesn't truly matter, as the result is the same: a divorce has occurred or is occurring, and divorce sucks. I want you to get past the divorce and on with your new life. My experience has allowed me to figure out how moving on can happen for people, and how this moving on business can happen faster and easier. My wish is that anyone going through divorce not suffer one second longer than they absolutely have to.

As a coach, I know that *technically* divorce is NOT a game. Neither is driving, but driving has rules. You follow the rules, you get from Point A to Point B in good time, and safely. Yes, I know those rules are actually laws, but you get the point. When you abide by the laws of divorce, in this case the *rules*, you get the results you want and you get them faster, easier and better. Oh yes, and you are happier. I know you want to be happier. Don't you?

3

Also, as a coach, I'm here to give you the tools you need to take ownership, stewardship and control of your life after divorce. I also want you to be happier and at peace, and really really soon. Doesn't that sound lovely? I know, right? Keep reading.

Who are you?

You are getting ready to file for divorce, going through a divorce, or your divorce is final and you still haven't truly moved past it.

You are tired, anxious, frustrated, sad, angry, or hurt … or all of the above. And, you're darn tired of it and you want to *feel better*. Heck, wouldn't it be great to feel great? Yes, that <u>can</u> happen.

You want someone to tell it like it is, not better than it is or worse, just as it is. You want to hear what in the world needs to get done so you can get unstuck, unrestricted, un-pissed-off, and free so you can move on with your life in a new, different and really awesome way … and the sooner the better.

If this is you, this is your book. Keep reading.

But I know from experience not everyone is ready to move forward. Some people like being pissed off and resentful.

If you are just fine, thank you very much, with plotting revenge against your ex, fantasizing about his demise, and can't wait until the next time you can discuss with your golf buddies what she did "this time," return this book immediately and perhaps pick it up again when you're tired of feeling like crap and you're ready to move forward. If you have done a

Google search recently for "where to hide the body," this just isn't the book for you. It doesn't matter if your divorce happened last week or in 1976, if you're still holding any resentment, anger or any other negative feeling toward your ex, guilt, sadness or anger within yourself, this is a book you will benefit from reading. I'm not going to sugar coat divorce and how to get through yours, even though I *am* an optimist. What I'm going to do is help you to think differently about what your divorce can mean to you, and what kind of life full of awesome-sauce you can create post-divorce with some tools, strategies, inner reflection, personal development and a positive mental attitude.

Yes, I did say awesome-sauce.

Chapter One:
Rule #1: You Will Survive and Be Just Fine

"Not to spoil the end for you, but everything is going to be okay. You're going to love your life after divorce." ~Honorée Corder

Divorce is not the end, or the beginning, *it is both*. Divorce marks the end of a marriage, and the beginning of what could be an amazing new life – your amazing new life. Let us get straight to the great news, shall we? The great news is you get to choose, design, and create a life of your choosing after divorce.

As we have already established, the process of divorce is downright awful. Regardless of whether you were the plaintiff or the defendant, resistant or relieved about the divorce, the process of going through a divorce is, very simply, *awful*.

Now, you may have been the one who finally pulled the plug and initiated proceedings. You may be more excited than depressed. But unless you're truly cold-hearted, you have feelings of regret, sadness, residual love for your former spouse, and probably some empathy.

Perhaps you were surprised when you were served with papers. Your ex didn't discuss their unhappiness with you at all, and without warning or even a sign,

7

you found yourself on the receiving end of their petition. Then I'll bet you're all sorts of hurt and angry right now.

She's found someone new and seems ambivalent to your feelings. You just separated two weeks ago and already he's in Cabo with his new girlfriend. The divorce was finalized on a Thursday and by that Saturday he was eloping at the courthouse. She's got the candles lit and the wine poured for what looks to be quite the evening, even as you're picking up the kids for the weekend.

Even worse, you're still connected to your ex on Facebook and get to see each breaking-news moment as it happens. *Go ahead and un-friend and block him or her right now. It's okay, I'll wait.*

Regardless of which side you're on, no matter what is happening right now or where you are in the divorce process, here's what you need to know:

There's a Light at the End of the Tunnel, and It's Not an Oncoming Train

Said differently, at some point in the future, and with quite a bit of work on your part, you can look back on this time and see it as the blessing it truly is.

And again, for those just tuning in: *You will survive and be just fine.*

In a perfect world, the one I live in in my head, you will *thrive!*

Let me tell you some more good news, and I promise there will be lots and lots of good news in this book, I rarely meet anyone who regrets going through divorce. While *to a divorced person* they agree divorce is a miserable process that takes too long, hurts beyond description, and costs too much, the only thing they wish they could truly change was when it happened. Yes, ladies and gentlemen, those who have gotten divorced and lived to tell the tale wish it would have actually happened sooner.

Even those whose spouses made the decision for them emphatically share their divorce was one of the best things that happened to them. If you're not quite there in your mind, I'm sure you're wondering how that can possibly be. I assure you "a divorce is a blessing in disguise" is what I continually hear, and what I've heard over and over again. I even heard that very sentence before my own divorce was final!

What are Your Options?

When going through a divorce, you've got options: You can be mad and stay mad. For years. *Forever.*

You can make sure the divorce take years and years, drags on and on, and cost lots of money.

You can be in denial. You were just relieved it was over, and other than that, "you're good."

You can punish your ex, and yourself, by exacting revenge and causing as much hurt as possible.

Or … you can change what you can change, accept what you cannot change, heal what needs healing, and have the courage to design the life you want.

The question on the table right now is: what are you going to do? Stay stuck, or let go and move on? The choice, indeed, is yours. All yours.

Turn Your Breakup Into Your Breakthrough

You're still here, so from this moment on I'm going to talk to you with the assumption you want to use your divorce as the launch pad for your new life. Even if you're still in the midst of it, you can start today making small and simple actions that will eventually result in the significant outcome *and life* you truly desire.

But first, and I know I promised a ton of great news {and there is an actual ton, I promise}, we must address the inevitable *breakdown* that is likely to occur, if it hasn't already. Not to sound flippant or dismissive, and I'm not talking about the kind of breakdown that will land you in an institution. I'm focused on the breakdown one has before their breakthrough, the one that makes you wonder if you're really losing it. The same breakdown that brings with it overwhelming feelings that can sometimes take over at the least-opportune moment, literally seconds after you've been really in a great mood. If you haven't had any of that happen yet, you probably will. You are grieving the end of your marriage, even if you are quite deliriously happy it's finally over!

Bookmark this page for when your breakdown happens, and read this again at that time:

- **Let your feelings out!** Be sure not to fight or stuff your feelings. It is completely normal to have lots of emotional ups and downs, and

10

feel many conflicting emotions, including anger, resentment, sadness, relief, fear, frustration, and confusion. Sometimes all in the same day! It's important to identify and acknowledge these feelings. While these emotions will often be painful, trying to suppress or ignore them will only prolong your grieving process.

- **Talk about how you're feeling**. Even if it is difficult for you to talk about your feelings with other people, it is very important to find a way to do so when you are grieving. We will discuss therapy and other types of support, but for now find someone to talk to, as knowing that others are aware of your feelings will make you feel less alone with your pain and will help you heal. Journaling can also be a helpful outlet for your feelings. Note: In some states, journals are discoverable during a divorce. Several attorneys consulted on this book recommended writing a journal *to your attorney* as a daily log. It will be protected under attorney-client privilege, even if you attorney never sees it.

- **Remember: moving on is your end goal**. Expressing your feelings will liberate you, and only a few times, to the right people, is probably enough. It is important not to dwell on the negative feelings or to over-analyze the situation. Getting stuck in hurtful feelings like blame, anger, and resentment will rob you of the valuable positive energy you need to heal and move forward.

- **Remember: you really do have an amazing future ahead of you.** When you commit to another person, you create many hopes and dreams. It's hard to let these dreams go. As you grieve the loss of the future you once envisioned, be encouraged by the fact that new hopes and dreams will eventually replace your old ones.

- **Know the difference between a normal reaction to a divorce, and real depression.** Grief can be paralyzing during and after a divorce. I promise that, after a while, the sadness begins to lift. Day by day, and little by little, you start moving on, feeling better, and having hope. However, if you don't feel any forward momentum even with these suggestions, you may be suffering from real depression and need to consult a therapist. We're going to touch on therapy in Chapter 2.

As you allow yourself to dream again, as you let the old dreams that came with your marriage go, you will feel your breakthrough happen. You will notice the sun on your face, the birds singing, even a butterfly or two. You will wake up and realize, *"Hey, I'm actually feeling pretty good today."*

I remember not being able to understand how the end of a relationship actually felt like physical pain. I couldn't wrap my brain around how a non-physical event literally physically hurt. It was awful. Yet I just kept putting one foot in front of the other, just kept doing what I knew would help me get better and feel better, and one day I woke up and hurt a little less. Months went by and I hurt even less. Then, my breakthrough happened and I actually *laughed out loud.* If it's been awhile for you, I totally get it. And, you will laugh again soon.

Start Right Where You Are and Begin to Determine Where You Want to Go

I'm always really excited to talk about creating a vision, which is the "where you want to go" part. Your divorce wound might be pretty fresh, so figuring out what you want your life to look like, and including other new people in that vision, might be a bit much right now. Stay with me. We're going to address creating an amazing vision in Chapter 5.

If you've been divorced for a *long* time, don't be too hard on yourself if it's taken this long to pick up a book to help you get on with gettin' on. Be patient with yourself, your process, and your healing.

Or, It Might Be Time for a Shower

If you are this far into the book and thinking, *"But Honorée, I'd be doing good right now to get in a daily shower,"* you're not alone. I remember thinking that any minute I would feel better, feel like doing something other than sleeping, watching television, and reading books to my daughter.

A very close friend of mine is freshly divorced, and until recently, he was having a super hard time. Sam[*] reported for more than two weeks in a row he was not accomplishing anything, and on some days, he didn't even get dressed, let alone take a shower. To further "assist" him in staying stuck, he's self-employed. He doesn't *need* to leave his home office on most days. In

---

[*] Not his real name.

fact, on days he doesn't have client calls or meetings, or a business development event, he has no reason to go into his home office. So, after he sent daughter off to school, he'd make a cup of coffee, read the news, and watch television. The television watching went on for hours, in fact, until it was time to make dinner for his daughter or, if she was busy or at her mom's, until it was time for bed.

The thought of crafting a long-term vision was overwhelming. He first had to create a short-term, day-long vision. Our conversations revealed that on days he had appointments, and he had to get up and shower, he actually felt better. In fact, as an extrovert, he refuels and replenishes by being around people. So staying at home perpetuated his inaction, because being alone didn't give him the energy he needs to get going.

Through a series of coaching conversations, we "engineered circumstances" to ensure he put something on his schedule every single day to ensure he would shower, get dressed, leave the house, and be around people. By going to an exercise Bootcamp a couple of days a week, Sam got his juices flowing and felt better because he started looking better. Having a lunch meeting a few days a week helped him access the part of him he knew was solid: his business mind. Setting networking coffees and going to events helped him to find new business, which by default, made sure he went into his home office.

Emotion is created by motion, and getting out helped him to feel energized. Being around people helped him to recharge his reserves. Those two combined gave him the capacity to begin to do things he had been putting off doing.

14

If you are going into the office just fine every day, you still might be stuck because work is *all* you're doing.

If you don't work outside of your home, then it's really easy to stay in your pajamas or sweats every single day.

My point is this: start right where you are, and give yourself something to do every day. Meet a friend for lunch or drinks. Take a yoga or spin class. Have a guys' night out ... or a girls' night out. Join a new organization for business or pleasure. Start a book club. Take up a new positive hobby like running, hiking, knitting, or learning a language (as opposed to a negative hobby like drugs or excessive drinking). Give yourself something to do, other than focusing on the past and why, some days, you feel like crap. Okay? Okay.

Moving On:
Your Action Steps for Moving Forward

*Un-friend, block, and disconnect with your ex on social media. Unless and until you're on **great** terms, you don't need to see what they are doing, and vice versa.
*Decide right now to choose your best option: *let go and move on.*
*Turn your breakup into your breakthrough by starting to dream about the future again.
*Get into the shower! Or take the next logical step to create a new, positive emotion through motion.

"Thinking you can unleashes the force that allows it to happen." ~Honorée Corder

Chapter Two:
Rule #2: You Must Assemble the Right Team and Get Support

*"Surround yourself with people who
think you're more awesome than sliced bread."*
~Honorée Corder

It's All About You Now

Life post-divorce is *all about you.* For the first time in a long time, what you want, when you want it, how you want it, and why you want what you want isn't about another person. It's about you.

I recently met Patricia, divorced just two weeks, clearly wearing her divorce on her face and in her heart. She was abused and mistreated by her spouse for more than 20 years. She finally got the courage to divorce him after she discovered years of infidelity and could no longer hope or pray it would get better; she certainly couldn't "make it work." When we talked, it was all about her ex. *He's doing this. He's going here. He's going there. He's got a girlfriend who thinks she's the kid's new mom.*

I encouraged her to begin to worry about herself, and only herself. Forget about her ex-husband and what he's doing. Communicate with him only when necessary (i.e., regarding visitation), and if civil verbal communication wasn't possible, only in writing via text, email or through her attorney.

I'm encouraging you to do the same: put your ex out of your mind, and in the past where he or she belongs, as much as humanly possible. Then, put yourself right smack in the forefront of your mind and thoughts.

Let's address first things first.

Your Story

Your new life and what you're creating starts right now. Well, sort of. As I just said, first things first, my friend! You've got to get what *has* happened all out. First you must tell the story of what happened, from your perspective, in your marriage. I want you to feel and know you have been heard, really heard, by someone that matters to you, understands you, and can help you heal, move through the hurt and anger your divorce has and is placing in your life, and move on. Even if that person is only you.

If you don't feel you were heard in your marriage, you may have stopped talking. Or, you may have just stopped talking to your spouse.

You have multiple options to get your story out:

- Write it. Get a journal or create a new document on your computer. Tell the story from beginning to end, in the time doses that work best for you.
- Record it. Use a smartphone app or even a digital recorder to record your story.
- Tell it. In individual or group therapy, share your story.

Note: Telling your story isn't for anyone else. No one else ever needs to read it, hear it, or know about it. Just you and the person or people you confide in.

Note well: Once you have told your story, in full, let it be the very last time you tell your story.

What do I mean?

I bet you've told pieces of your story over and over and over again, sometimes to help you process through what happened, sometimes to garner sympathy, and sometimes just to throw your ex under the bus, release some anger and make yourself feel better.

Let me ask you a hard question: *Did you really feel any better at all?* I bet you actually felt worse. I don't know about you, but right after my divorce, when I focused on the details of my failed marriage, I just got all fired up again. I was angry about how he treated me, frustrated I had put up with it, and really mad at myself for choosing him in the first place. I was sad because the relationship failed. And, I was a little hurt because he moved on right away.

Mostly, though, I was relieved to be out of the marriage and felt instantly better to not be in that environment any longer. And, of course, I thought I was "old and undesirable," being a smidge over 30 with a small child. As it turns out, I was wrong (more on that later).

Back to you: telling your story, once and finally, is about you, your healing, and creating the open space you need to move forward.

"Okay, coach," I can hear you say, *"how exactly do I go about this* 'It's all about me' *stuff."* No worries, I've got your back. Take a moment and grab something to write on or in, such as a notebook or

19

journal. We're going to take the first of some ever-so-important motion-creates-emotion action steps right now to ignite you.

Step 1: Take inventory.

In order to move forward, you've got to know where you are right now. Let's call where you are right now Point A. Point A is your "so what, now what" place in time. If by chance you look at your answers to the following questions and feel less than excited, that's perfectly normal and completely fine. In order to know the distance between where you are and where you're going to end up, you simply must know where you're starting. These questions offer you a true understanding of where you are right now, and help you to determine where you want to go. Nothing more, nothing less.

- Describe your life now (home environment, friendships, relationship status, etc.). If you want, you can also describe your Point A for your work/career.
- List the accomplishments, personally and professionally, you are most proud about, and go back as far as you'd like.
- List everything and everyone you are grateful for. Based on your current results, describe what is and has been working in your life and work.
- What's not working that now or eventually, you would like to be different?
- What do you need to let go of or stop doing? What else is not working?
- Write down everything and everyone you're grateful for in your life right now.

You're done for now. Take a deep breath. What did you discover? Are you in a pretty decent place? Or, are there lots of thing you want to improve? I will bet you have *many* things to be thankful for, and on top of that, a lot of clarity!

When you're ready, keep going:

Step 2: Create a new story.

Most people finish the exercise above with two basic realizations: it's not as bad as I thought, and I have a long way to go.

Regardless of where you are on the continuum, I have more of the afore-promised good news for you: you get to choose where you are going to go from here.

Now, let's pull everything together. You've already created your vision {haven't you?}, and now you're going to use that vision to create your new story.

Write down, as though writing a fiction novel, the new story of your life. Draw on your vision to complete the details, and you'll be telling your future story … only today, as if it is already real today.

When will you use this story, you ask? Anytime someone asks you how you're doing, or how things are going.

The challenge with going through a divorce is once people around you know you're going through a divorce, they are almost constantly asking, *"How are you today?"* to which the natural response is: *"Terrible. I'm going through a divorce! Wait until I tell you what she did yesterday …"*

21

Whoa! I'm sure you can see how that is going to contribute to you staying mad, sad, and stuck.

Once you've created this new story, you can say, *"I'm really excited about this new awesome life I'm creating in the future."*

You won't get sympathy, and people won't stop what they are doing to rush over and comfort you. If the secondary payoff you've received during the divorce has been the time and attention of people, then you need to recognize this sympathy and attention-getting behavior needs to come to a screeching halt. Once you seem fine, those who have dropped everything to bring you dinner or take you out for a cocktail will go back to their normal lives, and that's okay. You will go back to being treated "normally" because the perception will be that you're back to normal. You won't be, but you'll actually be on the path to better. It takes courage to say *no* to the drama and *yes* to your amazing future.

Finalize your first draft of your new story, then get busy talking about it – to yourself, your best friends, your colleagues, and anyone else who asks. If you haven't already, getting some clarity around your future direction should cause you to feel pretty excited.

Note: It's not that you're now "all better" and won't need to talk about your marriage, divorce, and current life. Your new story is for *most* of the people around you. In just a few pages, we'll uncover the appropriate places to process your past and work on your healing.

If you haven't written your story, then let me ask you this: which feels better to you? Feeling like crap focusing on the end of your marriage, or feeling amazing focusing on, and anticipating, your exciting future?

Go ahead, you can start writing right now.

You Must A-S-K to G-E-T

Once you've created your future vision and new story, you're going to need help. More than one thousand times, I've received an email or had a coaching conversation that included these words,

"One of the hardest things for me to do is ask for help."

If you don't *ask* for help, most likely you will not *get* any help. In other words, you must indeed a-s-k to g-e-t.

Designing your new life takes help. Healing your past takes help. Either way you slice it, sparky, if asking for help is a tough one for you, you're going to need to build your "asking" muscles.

Let me let you in on what is apparently a big secret: people love to help people they like and love. If I can do something to make the life of my husband, daughter, friends, or family easier, I am all in.

To go one step farther, you don't actually do very much all by yourself. You have the help of thousands of people you don't know, every single day. These are the folks that built your car, grew, harvested, transported, and put food on your table, made your clothes, built your house, and invented your smartphone.

Get my point? You asked for most of their help with your checkbook and AMEX™ card, yet you still asked for help.

Drilling this down a little closer to home, we all need help to make our lives work and work well.

If you're one of the people I'm talking about, and asking for help is commensurate to getting a root canal, I respectfully request you begin asking for the help you need, as early as today.

- Stop doing everything and start asking your assistant to schedule those appointments, file those documents, and send those emails.
- Stop running errands and take your mom up on her offer to do them for you.
- Stop holding all of your emotions in and start asking those who care enough to ask how you are to listen when you need to talk.

You can ask your son to take out the garbage or to help you do it. You can ask your sister to take the dog to the vet for shots, instead of stressing over taking time off from work. There are so many opportunities, most of them small and simple, to ask those around you for assistance.

As you're moving through divorce into your new life, you'll have even more opportunities to ask for the specific help you need from the very people who can give it to you. First, you need to be able to ask.

Your assignment is to look for opportunities to ask for help and actually ask for it. The response is inconsequential, although most of the time, you'll probably get a resounding "yes!" Your focus is, as we've discussed, on you. You're building your asking muscles, nothing more or less.

Who's On Your Bench?

"Your inner circle determines your outer circumstances." ~Honorée Corder, Vision to Reality

As you're running all over creation, finally asking for help, you might be noticing the changing faces in your life.

Some of the people you thought were your best friends will suddenly get the "divorce flu" and you won't hear from them, and you'll see them less and less, if at all. The divorce flu is what some of your married friends get when you announce your separation because they are afraid that your divorce is something they can "catch," which will cause them to get divorced, too.

Some people will have a limited capacity to support you. They won't go away, because perhaps they've been your friend since the earth cooled, or they are related by blood, but they will definitely keep their distance.

Then there are those who will show up for you in a way that surprises you in a good way.

Finally, you will meet some new and great people on your divorce journey.

I'm a firm believer in the power of environment. Said another way, who you have in your life, and the things you have surrounding you, determine whether or not you succeed. In this case, whether or not you heal and succeed in creating a life you love after divorce. Harsh? Perhaps. True? Absolutely. You see, your environment -- comprised of your home, your workplace, your friends and associates -- determines with great accuracy whether you will be successful ... or not.

As I was navigating a challenging time in my business about a decade ago, I received a destiny-changing phone call from a respected business colleague. He asked me a particularly powerful question, one of the best I have ever heard: *Do you realize that success in life is determined not in who you hire, but in who you fail to fire?"*

That question prompted me to revisit my vision of my ultimate desired friends: who I really wanted to spend time with and invest my time in, and what I would expect of them and of myself in our ongoing relationship.

Not very long after I received the first call, another powerful call changed my trajectory. Another long-time friend asked me the mother of all power questions: *"Who do you have in your life asking you a better question every single day, challenging you to be the best you can be?"*

She knew how easy it would be for me to stay on my comfortable, current path, smack dab in the middle of my comfort zone, completely ignore my restlessness, and become complacent.

At the time, while I had some loving and wonderful people around me, the number of people challenging me to be my best on a daily basis was almost non-existent. I was still in the process of getting a divorce and thinking a lot about the next chapter of my life. I realized that in order to take my life to the next level, I needed a level of support that did not exist for me. I needed to find more people living the life I aspired to live, who would be willing to push me, pull me, entice me and encourage me each and every day. With my friend's encouragement, that of my coach, and a few other close friends, I made some crucial decisions that literally changed my destiny.

Once I stepped through the fear and made the decisions I needed to make, everything fell into place. It will for you, too.

The two questions above, at exactly the right times in my life, gave me ultimate clarity. They pointed out to me that the choices I was making in my relationships and business were holding me back, and not allowing me to move forward.

How does this relate to you? Perhaps the people around you don't bring out the best in you. They don't challenge you to expect results you think may be impossible. They could be in your life more by default than design.

Taking Inventory

Now is the perfect time to take a complete inventory of the people in your life. A life by design includes intentionally thinking through who is in your life, who you want to have in your life, and in what capacity.

I have three basic categories in my life: the intimate circle, the inner circle, and everybody else.

Intimate Circle

The intimate circle, my intimate circle, as you might imagine, consists of my husband, daughter, some family members, and my besties. These are the people who know me the best, know pretty much every little thing about me and love me anyway. They love and encourage me unconditionally. I trust them implicitly and know I can rely on them, in good times and in not so good times. These are the people who are the first to hug and listen when I'm upset, buy my books when they are released, and help me hide the bodies. {Just kidding.}

Deciding to include someone in the *intimate circle* is a choice that can, and will, affect how happy, successful and fulfilled you will be in almost every area of your life. In other words, choose wisely.

Not to point out the obvious, but had we {as in you *and* me} chosen our spouses better, I wouldn't be writing this book and you wouldn't be reading it. No need for healing, therapy, or hefty attorneys' fees. Because we're turning lemons into lemonade here, we're going to focus on what's to come, and who is going to go on the ride of our new lives with us.

Inner Circle

Your inner circle will contain, as does mine, close friends, *other* family members, and perhaps some non-colleagues at work.

You trust these people, and they are a wonderful addition to your life. They round out the list of people you consider close to you. They support you in your endeavors.

The difference between the intimate circle and the inner circle comes down, quite simply, to *time* and *trust*. It's not that the inner circle folks couldn't be in the intimate circle. You simply don't have either the time to get them in there, or you feel like there is a barrier to the amount of trust you can extend to them. That's not meant in a negative way, it just simply is what it is. I see some people once every few years. We are close, yet they don't get the daily blow-by-blow of my happenings.

These are the people who you'll invite to your next wedding, your 40th birthday party, even your kid's graduation. You connect several times a year and you feel comfortable being your authentic self with them.

Everyone Else

And then, there's everyone else. Anyone who isn't in the intimate or inner circles falls into the "everyone else" category. These people, in my life, are on a need-to-know basis. Frankly, they don't need to know much. I'm a positive and somewhat public person, and while that's who I am *most* of the time, the rest of the world just simply won't know when I'm under the weather, dealing with PMS (mine or my daughter's), or having any kind of life challenge. They just won't, and here's why: it's not that you don't care, *it's that you don't care.* Right?

We can't assume everyone wants to hear about our drama and personal or professional problems. As humans, we only have the capacity to care about a finite amount of stuff, and our own stuff is at the top of our list. The people who care, truly care, about what's going on with you good, bad or indifferent, are the folks that sit, you guessed it, on the intimate circle list. Some are on the inner circle list, but none of them are on the everyone else list.

If you've been telling everyone your tragic story of divorce and unfortunate life events, save it from now on for the people who really care, or the people you pay to care … like your therapist and your coach.

The rest of the time, have a smile on your face and let people wonder what's really going on with you!

Your Action:

Going forward, thoughtfully and intentionally choosing who gets the coveted spots in your intimate circle must be done with as much forethought and prudence as you can muster.

Time to grab your journal and make a list of everyone in your life. Carefully and with much deliberation, categorize each person as *Intimate Circle, Inner Circle, Everyone Else*.

Don't worry so much if the first two lists are really, really short. That is okay and, especially after a divorce, pretty normal. If you're lucky enough to have a substantial number of great people on both lists, count your blessings and be thankful.

You'll obviously spend the majority of your time with your intimate and inner circle people. It is entirely possible, no *probable*, that some of the people in your life who had positions on either of those two lists will need to be re-categorized and put onto the everyone else list. *"How do I do this?"* you say? You don't need to call each person up, tell them they aren't quite cutting the mustard and inform them they are being relegated to a new category.

You're simply going to let them go, mentally first and then in actuality. It's easier than you think. Haven't you meant to call someone for weeks, sometimes months at a time, and then eventually it's been more than a year and you feel embarrassed even considering making the call. Heck, you've been meaning to do lots of things, maybe even for years, you haven't gotten around to doing. Life has gotten in the way ... work has been hectic, the kids have a ton of activities, then the holidays and, of course, the divorce process has been more complicated and time-consuming than you anticipated. You just haven't had time to call. Or visit. Or have lunch or coffee. Right? Right.

My dear friend and mentor, Pam Chambers, used to advise me to "paint it red" if I ever wanted to own a situation. "I haven't called because I've been busy but that's no excuse, so here I am after three years. How are you?"

You're going to do the opposite of painting it red. There's no need to hurt someone's feelings or be a jerk about cutting ties or limiting contact. It is what it is, and that's all it is.

During this time, it's important to take control of your physical environment, and here's why:

You'll suddenly have tons more energy. As you let go of the items that no longer serve you or feel good to have in your life, such as furniture, jewelry, clothing and "tchotchkes," you will notice you feel lighter and happier. Things will happen faster, easier, and better than ever before.

31

You will be much more creative. Letting go of people and things, not to mention feelings, allows any creative juices that seemingly had dried up to come alive again.

You'll create synergy with the old and new people in your life, which will automatically take you higher.

You'll have much less stress. As you streamline the details of your life, you get rid of the old baggage and create more room for new and exciting opportunities.

In coaching, I talk a lot about "tolerations" with my clients. Tolerations are those things that zap your energy, annoy you, and drain away your effectiveness, happiness and success. They make you less attractive to yourself, and therefore, less attractive to others. Tolerations can be people, things, situations, events, even our marriages and jobs!

You have three choices with tolerations: change them, eliminate them, or accept them.

Your environment, including the people in it, is crucial to your success or failure. Think about each person in your life: are they supportive of your vision and your goals? Do they ask you empowering, and if necessary, tough questions? Or do they predict failure, doom, or worse? Be aware of what your friends, family, and associates bring to your life. If they are not empowering you to be your best, perhaps it is time for them to go! As I mentioned, you won't need to necessarily usher people out of your life, quit your job, or burn the entire house down and start over. To maintain your sanity, keep your distance from the people who drain you. Look at it this way: there are many people you want to stay in touch with, people you admire and those are the people you'll make time for as often as you can. Allow the relationships that are no longer in your best interest to fade away. It's that easy.

In addition, fearlessly give away, throw away, or donate items you don't absolutely love. I know for a fact you won't miss the items you let go of, and you will relish in the extra mental and physical space you've created.

By taking control of your immediate environment, you reclaim your personal power and set a healthy and focused foundation for your future.

Now that you've gotten a firm hold on your current environment, the time has come to get the help you need from some new team members who can rock your world in a fantastic and delicious way.

The Big Three:
Your Attorney, Your Therapist, & Your Coach

The divorce team you have surrounding you during and immediately following your divorce is critical to both your success and your sanity. If you've been divorced for a while, you know exactly what I mean: the wrong attorney can cost you dearly, financially and emotionally. An ineffective therapist can prolong your agony without measurable results. And, I can promise you that you don't want to miss out on the benefits of having a divorce coach.

Your Attorney

One of the most important decisions you will make in your divorce process is choosing the right attorney. Being represented by a skilled attorney can mean the difference between a relatively smooth divorce and a divorce marked by frustration, delay, wrong turns, and preventable negative results. You want to make certain that your attorney has the skill, the experience, and the temperament to effectively represent you. You also want to make sure that your attorney has good professional relationships with other lawyers, with the local Judges, and with the Court personnel. You don't want to hire an attorney that causes the Judge to say to herself "Not this lawyer again!" So beyond typing "divorce attorney [insert city]" into Google, how do you find your personal advocate?

1. Collect the Names of Several Attorneys

You would not buy a house without attending several open houses and having the house inspected by a contractor. You would not purchase a new pair of shoes before trying them on. You certainly should not choose a divorce attorney, the very expert who will counsel you through one of your most significant life changing experiences, before researching, meeting, and interviewing several candidates. Here are a few ways to get the names of attorneys to interview:

- **Personal Recommendations.** Ask a close friend who recently went through a divorce about her experiences with her attorney. If your friend was satisfied with her attorney, ask her why. What was it about her lawyer that she found to be effective? Competent? Comforting? If your friend was not satisfied with her attorney, would she recommend her husband's? Also, if your friend did not have a good experience with her own divorce attorney, ask her why. In either event, her experiences will be beneficial to you in selecting your own divorce attorney. You should also seek referrals through connections at work, church, and through friends and friends of friends.

- **Professional Referrals.** Attorneys in different areas of practice can usually provide the names of divorce attorneys they trust. For instance, trusts and estates attorneys often have close relationships with divorce attorneys, so contact the attorney who wrote your will, trust, or other estate documents. Everybody knows a lawyer, so if you have a lawyer friend or a professional colleague who is a lawyer, ask the person if they know a good divorce attorney. If your lawyer friend works for a law firm, ask him or her to make an inquiry at her law firm for a recommendation. Other good referral sources include CPAs, financial advisors, therapists, and counselors. These professional people often work closely with lawyers. They also work with clients that are divorcing or who have been divorced, and therefore will be able to provide useful information about divorce attorneys.

- **Websites.** As a last resort, try professional websites. This option will take longer and you won't have a way to initially verify that the attorney is competent. Trusting your gut in this particular situation can go either way. If relying on the internet, here are a few tips. First, determine if your state has Specialization Certifications for divorce attorneys. States such as California and Texas have Boards of Legal Specialization that offer certifications for qualified divorce attorneys. You can find this information through the

State Bar in the state in which you live. For instance, in the State of Texas there are more than 70,000 lawyers, but only 700-800 Board Certified family law attorneys. If you live in a state that offers Board Certification or other specialization certification for divorce attorneys (usually under the specialization "family law"), you can narrow the search to the city or county in which you live. The next avenue is to search for a lawyer through the American Academy of Matrimonial Attorneys ("AAML"), a prestigious organization of family law attorneys. The website is www.aaml.org. The AAML website can direct you to qualified divorce attorneys in your area. Next, Super Lawyers, a website and magazine that selects top attorneys in each city based on peer reviews, evaluations and third party research, allows you to search for an attorney by state and practice area. The website is www.superlawyers.com.

However, you should be cautious about selecting a lawyer based upon online rating websites. One dissatisfied client can tarnish the reputation of an otherwise exceptional divorce lawyer. On the other hand, one praiseworthy review can unrealistically seemingly elevate a lawyer who may not be competent. Finally, you should check with the State Bar in your state to determine if the lawyer you are researching has ever been sanctioned or disciplined by his or her State Bar for any disciplinary matter. In conclusion, no matter what websites and online research you undertake, you should be very cautious about selecting a lawyer based only upon online research.

2. Vet Attorneys You Plan to Interview

Once you have narrowed your list of prospective attorneys by doing your pre-meeting research, Google the attorney and check out his or her website, Facebook or LinkedIn page if available. Read about the lawyer, his or her firm, his or her education, background, and focus area of practice. Some other things to look for in your research:

- Is the attorney part of a firm that has other divorce attorneys? Does the attorney practice in a law firm that only handles divorce and family law cases?

- Does your attorney practice only matrimonial or other types of law as well? In my opinion, you definitely want a specialist: someone who focuses her practice in family and matrimonial law only.

3. Interview Them in Person

A brief phone conversation can help determine if it is worthwhile to set up an initial, in-person consultation, saving you (and the attorney) time. A lawyer or someone from her office should return your call promptly. If the attorney or her assistant takes several days to return the call, you should be cautious. Most family law attorneys have told me that they return phone calls the same day or they call the next day offering an apology. Even if the attorney is on vacation, in trial, or recovering from major surgery, someone from his office should still either take your call or return your call promptly. If the attorney is not available, make sure that you ask to speak to his assistant. It is also appropriate to ask the receptionist when you can expect a return phone call.

The initial phone call is also a good time to ask about fees. Most divorce attorneys charge by the hour but require a retainer, a fee charged in advance to cover the initial hours they will work on your case. Retainers vary widely by location, but can range from $1,000.00 in a small town to $50,000.00 or more in larger cities. If the amount of the retainer makes you cringe, you probably cannot afford that attorney. If the attorney is beyond your price range, ask him or her to recommend a more affordable attorney at another firm, something the attorney should be willing to provide.

You should also ask if there will be a fee for the initial consultation. Some lawyers charge a fee for their initial consultation, and other lawyers do not. If you cannot afford the lawyer's fee for the initial consultation, you probably cannot afford the lawyer.

Don't be surprised if the preliminary phone call is with the attorney's assistant. Many lawyers train their assistants to provide and receive information, including information about fees, prior to the face-to-face meeting.

During the initial phone call, if it appears you can afford the lawyer's fees, you should arrange a face-to-face meeting.

You must make sure you have a carefully thought-out plan for funding your divorce. Just like every other service you buy, your attorney will expect you to keep your bills current. In other words, don't expect your attorney to keep working if you haven't paid your bill.

Divorce life is just like regular life: when you ask someone to perform work, you expect to pay for that work immediately or within a short-time period. Your divorce attorney is not different from any other professional, they rely on being paid on time and in full.

4.   The Interview

The main purpose of the in-person interview is to tell the attorney the basic facts of your case, hear his or her thoughts, and get an idea of his legal approach. Some attorneys are more confrontational in nature; others practice collaborative law. You want to choose the person who closely matches your style. Most initial consultations take between one and two hours. These are some of the questions that you want to ask in the initial consultation:

- Does the lawyer have experience practicing in front of this particular court? If so, what is the lawyer's experience with the court?
- If your husband's lawyer is known, has the lawyer you are interviewing had experience with your husband's lawyer? What should you expect?
- How often does the attorney go to court? How often does he take depositions?
- What is the policy about returning phone calls? When can you expect phone calls to be returned? Will you be given the lawyer's cell phone? His direct line?
- Ask to meet your lawyer's assistant. Ask if an associate attorney will be working on the case and, if so, ask to meet the associate.
- Does the lawyer prefer communication by e-mail or by telephone? Some lawyers receive several hundred e-mails a day, and it may be more effective for you to call the lawyer instead of sending an e-mail.

- Ask who will be handling the day-to-day issues of your case, and if it is not the attorney you interviewed (as is often the case), ask to meet the associate or colleague who will be helping.
- If there are court hearings or depositions scheduled, ask the attorney what he or she will be doing to prepare for those court hearings and depositions.
- Ask the attorney if an expert witness will need to be hired and who the lawyer would recommend (perhaps a child psychologist in a child custody case or a forensic accountant in a complex property case).
- Ask the lawyer if mediation is an option. In most cases, the court will require you to go to mediation, especially if children are involved. Ask about the costs of mediation. Ask the lawyer to explain the mediation process to you in detail.
- Ask the attorney how you will be billed. Will you be billed for every e-mail or every telephone call? Don't be surprised or offended if the answer is "yes" as the only thing that a lawyer has to sell is his or her experience, expertise, and time. It is always appropriate to ask the lawyer what you can do to minimize the costs and make things easier on the lawyer and his or her staff.

Red Flags: Signs the attorney you are interviewing is not for you:

1. The attorney makes promises or guarantees about the outcome of your divorce after hearing only your side of the story. A good divorce attorney knows there is no "sure

thing" in divorce, and he or she will be very careful to give you a realistic and honest appraisal of your case. A lawyer can never guarantee the result in any case, and one who does so should be viewed with skepticism. On the other hand, it is appropriate to ask your lawyer about the likelihood of a particular result, and the lawyer should give you an honest and candid answer. Be wary, however, of the lawyer that guarantees results.

2. The attorney drops the names of important or famous clients he or she has represented, and provides confidential details. If the attorney will tell you about others, they will tell others about you. Providing confidential information about any client, is a breach of a lawyer's professional ethics. You also should be extremely concerned if a divorce attorney is quick to provide you confidential information about his celebrity cases in an effort to impress you.

3. The attorney tells "war story" after "war story" of his or her past legal exploits in an apparent attempt to impress you. While it is always appropriate to ask the lawyer about his or her experience, it will be obvious to you when the lawyer goes from giving an honest appraisal of prior experience to boastful storytelling.

4. You don't get the attorney's full attention during the initial interview. Attorneys can be busy people. However, an attorney should give his or her full attention to a prospective client. Of course, sometimes there are matters that the attorney must attend to, but even then

he or she should tell you that in advance, for instance, "I am expecting a short phone call that I could only schedule at this time, so please forgive me for a few moments." Sometimes these things are unavoidable. With that said, the lawyer should listen carefully to you during the interview and provide you with his or her full attention.

5. The lawyer does not answer your questions. A good divorce lawyer will listen carefully to your question, provide you with an answer, and will typically ask, "Did I answer your question to your satisfaction?" If the lawyer dances around your question without giving an answer, or is unable to answer your questions concisely and intelligently, you should be concerned.

6. The lawyer tells you that he knows the judge or he speaks disrespectfully about the judge. There is knowing the Judge and then there is "knowing the Judge." Lawyers practice in front of judges. It is what they do. It is not uncommon for attorneys to pick up on and be familiar with the "do's" and "don'ts" of certain judges. You would expect this. However, you need to be wary of any lawyer that promises a result based upon some type of a "special" relationship with the judge. You also need to be concerned if the attorney speaks about the judge in a disrespectful or condescending manner. In both instances, the lawyer is showing disrespect for the judicial process in general and to the judge in particular, and you have to determine if you want such a person representing you in your divorce.

4. Make Your Choice

When it comes down to choosing an attorney out of the several you have interviewed, be more intuitive than scientific. Even if the attorneys you interviewed are all acceptable on paper, there is no guarantee each one will be a good fit. Go with your gut and choose the attorney that feels right. Divorce is a highly personal and emotionally charged process, so choose the attorney that you will feel comfortable sharing some of the more intimate details of your life.

If you have received strong recommendations, done your research and interviewed several candidates, you should find an attorney who will advocate for you, patiently answer your questions, and guide you through a difficult process.

Be sure to contact your attorney only regarding legal matters. Many of the attorneys I interviewed for this book shared they were frustrated with the number of calls they received from clients that did not address legal matters. This causes two problems: it markedly increases your bill, and prevents your attorney from making actual progress on your case. If you are constantly calling them and expecting them to listen to every drama-filled, non-legal detail of your case, they are constricted and unable to work efficiently and effectively on your behalf. They may eventually avoid your calls in order to focus on creating a solid work product, and when push comes to shove, they may fire you for making it too difficult to pursue the legal aspects of your matter.

What's your solution for processing the more challenging and non-legal issues of your divorce? I'm so glad you asked! You'll want to utilize the other two members of The Big Three: your therapist and your coach, to help you work through your wounds and provide tools for handling and creating your future.

Your Therapist

With a strong, supportive cast of characters, such as a mom and dad, siblings, and close friends, it's still almost impossible to navigate a divorce without also getting the help of someone who is not emotionally involved. Most likely those who know and love you are ill-equipped to help you successfully manage your daily challenges, deal with your long list of responsibilities, and handle the emotional roller-coaster. More likely, they are great at listening, lending an ear or a dollar now and then, and offering up a much-needed hug. They cannot, however, help you to move through your divorce in the way only trained professionals can.

If you're like me when I was going through my divorce, you have no family to speak of, and your closest friends live 1,000 miles away. If you have children, they want to know they are safe and loved, and they need additional support during this time of personal crisis.

While having an attorney is all but a necessity, going to therapy still has a bit of a stigma and isn't considered a non-negotiable. Much like having a coach, I think therapy should absolutely be part of your healing process.

If you are going through divorce without a strong support system, a solid set of boundary-setting tools, and a healthy self-esteem, I recommend therapy for you. If you "still" feel angry, resentful, or sad about your ex, therapy definitely could be helpful.

If your kids are asking questions you don't know how to answer, a therapist can bridge that gap. A therapist's office can provide a soft place to fall, a safe place to process what's happening, and provide you with some tools and strategies for dealing with your divorce, and get a handle on it.

Choosing Your Therapist

1. Ask Your Network

Much like finding an attorney, a personal referral can be the easiest, fastest, and most effective way to find a therapist. All three times I've engaged a therapist, they have been recommended through friends or family.

2. Shop Online

While I have never found a therapist online, I do think that in this day and age where we can find anything we want to know through Google, online is likely the way that most will first meet their therapist. You can search on Psychology Today's "Therapy Finder." When therapist shopping, I would look for therapists who are not selling themselves but rather seem to be trying to tell you about their work and their philosophy of working with patients.

3. Identify the Philosophy

Every therapist has a therapeutic philosophy that drives their practice, such as *unconscious motivation, cognitive, solution-oriented,* and *family systems.* As a systems person, I enjoy working with someone who gets to the root of the problem or situation, and provides a system {set of tools} I can actively use to deal with the root and put in place something better for the future. Two of my favorite therapists were *systems-based* and that worked well for me. You'll want to discover the style and philosophy that works best for you, and look for a therapist with that very philosophy.

4. More Interviewing

Interview more than one therapist. Notice how you feel as you sit in the room, discuss your story and feelings, and whether or not you feel heard. You have to feel 100% comfortable with a therapist or you won't be honest with him, and frankly, he won't be able to help you to the best of his ability.

The process of therapy, which you most likely will combine with personal growth and self-reflection during your divorce process, is not for the weak. Over time, however, you will get better, the intense emotions lessen, and you will get the hang of your new life. Before you know it, you will be feeling better, more like your old happy self or even better. The work is worth the effort!

Your Coach
Written with Certified DTCP™ Divorce Coach Chris St. Clair

During my divorce and numerous decree modifications, I would have been a better client and would have gotten a far better return on my investment had I hired a divorce coach. This is not a self-serving proclamation because I'm a divorce coach; I'm a divorce coach because this is true. I was drawn to this work because I wanted to serve those going through the process and those working through co-parenting issues. Business executives, professional athletes, world leaders, and men and women of all ages leverage coaches during good times and transitions to bring out the best of who they are and to help them reach their full potential. Divorce is the mother of all "transitions," so logically it is an optimal time for a coach.

Coaching is built on the premise that nothing is broken. After divorce, it is simply time to move forward rather than making the assumption that you're broken or the divorce has caused irreparable damage. Coach and client are a team and each bring vital information to the relationship. The focus is on personal growth, creating and achieving your vision and goals and eliminating the limiting beliefs that may be holding you back. During my divorce, a clear vision would have provided just the focus I needed to help me shift my attention from the frustration-of-the-day toward my desired future.

You may be saying, *"That's all well and good, but coaching sounds a bit too touchy-feely, and I'm spending my hard earned money on an attorney and other professionals to bring this divorce to a close. I don't need to spend more!"* If so, consider this: one sure way to get the most out of every dollar spent with your attorney is to be an effective decision maker, be at your best, and have a clear vision of your future throughout your divorce.

Your best self:

- Has a clear future vision;
- Knows what your family needs/wants;
- Knows the priority of your goals;
- Understands *why* you want what you want;
- Is an effective and productive problem solver;
- Is focused on harmony and moving forward not vengeance or greed.

So, *how* do you find and bring out your best self every day? Friends? Family? Therapy? Medication? Nope. In my experience, the most effective way to discover and hold on to your best self is to work with a divorce coach. Your coach will work *with* you, not on you, to understand your goals, to uncover your dreams, to help you define your vision and create a plan for your future. Your coach will work with you to gain insight to your inner truth-teller. The same voice in you who knows you best, knows what you are capable of accomplishing, the voice that fights against the status quo and wants the best for you. Your coach will also help you overcome your personal sabotaging beliefs; those inner messages that tell you why something can't be done and generally keeps you from moving forward. Most of all, your coach will be by your side to hold you accountable to the goals you set for yourself.

Let's use a real life example to illustrate this point:

Your attorney says, "We're set for court tomorrow and we're in agreement on the strategy right? We're going for standard visitation and child support, and a modified holiday and summer schedule due to the wishes of the children and past experiences. Whatever you do, don't let anything they say get to you. Remain calm and let me do the talking. Don't let them see you upset. That will only hurt your case."

You say, "Yes, I understand, and I'm ready."

Tomorrow arrives, and along with it allegations of poor parenting, manipulation of the children, that your dating behavior is bad for the children and a request that custody be modified due to your poor choices.

Additionally, a request is made that the children be brought into court to testify.

You do your best to remain calm, but upon hearing the request to bring the children in to the courtroom, you lose it and start defending against one allegation after another.

Sound familiar?

The judge weighs in: "Alright everyone, I've heard enough, clearly there is a lot going on in this case and much missing information. I need more data. I'm ordering a CPS (Child Protective Services) evaluation. We're adjourned until I get a report from CPS."

You have spent time, money, and emotion on a day in court that yielded nothing! In fact, you took a step backward. What if, instead of heading into court with little more than a plan and good intentions, you armed yourself with the proper tools? What's the old saying, "You don't take a knife to a gun fight?" That might be a bit graphic, but the message is clear: arm yourself with the tools to handle the situation you're in, not the situations you'd like to be in. You didn't hire a banker to handle your legal issues, you hired an attorney. Your attorney is the right "tool" for the legal aspects of your case. Now it's time to become the CEO of your life, by hiring a divorce coach and arming yourself with powerful tools to achieve your goals!

In this specific situation, the three tools your coach would focus you on would be:

1. What is the outcome you desire – a subset of your vision and goals?

49

2. What does the outcome give you (a.k.a. why is the outcome important to you) – based upon your values?

3. Who do you want to be in the situation – what version of yourself serves you best in this situation?

With these three questions to focus on, you have your "home base," your mantras to draw on when the waters of court or mediation get rough.

Here's more good news, as promised: a valuable by-product of arming yourself with situation-specific tools is the perspective shift that comes with knowing *you* are prepared and in control. There is a fundamental difference in perspective when you feel safe, secure, and in control of your destiny versus feeling at risk, insecure, and holding on by a thread. Think about an area of your life where you have ultimate confidence in yourself, such as work, parenting, gardening, or sports. Think about someone criticizing you in this area. Most criticism in this area will fall on your deaf ears right?! The tools above shift your perspective to a safe, secure, supported mindset and dramatically expand your deaf ear zone!

As I mentioned above, I wish I had hired a coach during my divorce. I tried therapy but, for me, therapy was only mildly helpful. This had far less to do with the power of therapy and far more to do with my needs. I spent many married years thinking through why I chose this man and how not to do this again. I was ready for future-focused conversations about what I wanted and how I was going to get it. The search was on for someone or something to help me bring my future vision into focus, create action plans to achieve my vision, and the big daddy of them all, something to make me stop second-guessing every step I took. I found the Personal Power series by Anthony Robbins. Rather than attend the "expensive" weekend seminar (it really wasn't expensive but I told myself I couldn't afford it), I opted for the self-paced series and workbook. It was effective in helping me (and I was able to use it time and again over the years), but I didn't give myself the gift of an advocate.

You see, all coaching styles and methodologies aside, one powerful thing you get with a coach is a personal advocate. This is not someone who tells you what you want to hear or that you're awesome and perfect; this is a person who tells you the truth. The truth may be hard to hear (especially if it's positive) but you can count on your coach to be by your side and call it like it is.

Choosing Your Coach

1. Ask Your Network

Coaches are an integral part of many industries and aid in the growth and development of individuals and corporations at all levels within the company and all stages of careers. Likewise, coaches are leveraged throughout the stages of life transitions from high school to college, college to first job, long-time position to new career (stay-at-home mom to paid career). Because coaches are highly leveraged in many industries, start your search for a coach with the people you know. Your network may have valuable insight to coaching referrals. Every coach I know believes strongly in the power of finding the right fit for each client. Coaching is a partnership (as noted earlier) so the fit must be there or your coach can't be your authentic advocate. With this in mind, even a coaching contact outside of your field could be a good contact because coaches know coaches. Be clear about what you want from coaching; ask for what you need and you may find that if a referral isn't the right fit for you, they may have a great referral for you!

2. Shop Online

There are some good coach search sources online. In some cases, such as Noomi.com, the service is free and provides matching services based upon your criteria/requirements. Be aware that some of these are paid services so the folks on the site have paid to be there. I point this out not to diminish the credentials of the professionals on these sites, but simply to note that there are many outstanding coaches who choose not to use these services. Another good option is the ICF (International Coaches Federation) site. Many cities have a local chapter with a directory of coaches and their focus areas. You can also use a general Google search by focus area, such as divorce coach, life coach, career coach, etc. and include your city. I have used both a local and long-distance coach and have coached folks both locally and long distance. Both are effective so it's purely a personal choice.

3. Coaches have focus areas and philosophies

Coaches typically choose focus areas based upon their skills and passion. As you search for a coach, you will find coaches with many focuses. Let this work for you as you find a coach to meet your needs. If you prefer a Christian divorce coach who will address your personal and spiritual needs, you can find one. If you have an artistic flare and need to connect with someone as expressive as you, then be sure to include this criterion in your search. If your career is a key element of your recovery plan, then find a coach who can address your personal and career needs.

Additionally, coaches come from many walks of life and follow different coaching philosophies. There are highly co-active coaches like myself, who believe that all of us are naturally creative, resourceful and whole (a cornerstone of the CTI ® model) and therefore coaching can only be successful when client and coach are fully committed to the client's personal growth and transformation. The Divorce Transformation Coaching Program™ (DTCP™), works from the same premise that the client possesses the power to make significant changes in their life while also providing a proven methodology to aid in recovery and transformation after divorce. The key is the coach/client relationship, creating new habits, and accountability. There's more information about the DTCP™ at the close of this book.

There are many coaching methodologies, so choose the methodology that best meets your needs, will get you the results you desire, and is in line with your values. One thing to watch for are the organizations who tell you that they are "the" or "the only" legitimate coaching approach. While I believe in the approach I use and I will talk to potential clients about why I use this approach, there is no single, national governing board for divorce coaches. The International Coaches Federation is the closest entity to a coaching governing body. Simply put, beware of anyone who focuses on what is wrong with someone else's approach versus focusing on you and whether or not the two of you are a good fit.

4. More Interviewing

I cannot stress enough how important it is to feel a connection with your coach. You need to feel heard, safe, and honored and your growth and personal transformation need to be the primary focus of the relationship. Having said that, any coach worth having is going to push you outside your comfort zone! While interviewing your new coach, be sure that the coach's motivational approach works for you. If the coach you are interviewing does not challenge or push you, you might be better off as friends. Do I need to say that again? You need to feel challenged and pushed in order to make forward progress. Interview multiple coaches, ask questions, and find the best fit for you!

Coaching is about moving forward, focusing on your future vision and achieving the goals you set for yourself. Action and forward momentum are the name of the game. If you are ready to create your future and live to your full potential, find your coach, and get started!!

Moving On:
Your Action Steps for Moving Forward

*Remember: *it's all about you now!*
*Take Inventory & Create a New Story
*Ask for the help you need.
*Put a great team on your bench: your intimate circle, inner circle, attorney, therapist, and divorce coach.

"Have the best people you can find on your bench, and you'll be thrilled with how supported you feel in your new life." ~Honorée Corder

Chapter Three:
Rule #3: You Must Heal and Forgive ... as Soon as Possible

*"You must forgive, not because forgiveness is
deserved, but because you deserve peace."*
~Honorée Corder

You Want Me to Forgive *Whom?*

There are at least two people I want you to work on
forgiving, and let's start with the most important one
first: you.

You might not think you need to forgive yourself, and
yet I know if you peel back a few layers of the onion,
you'll see you are most likely holding a grudge
against yourself. Let's be clear: you are the very
person who needs a soft place to fall right now, and
one of those soft places needs to be within you.

You may find, as I did, it was very easy to beat
yourself over the head about the "if only's" and
"should have's" of your relationship.

- *If only* I had listened to my gut and not gone
  through with the marriage.
- I *should have* been more affectionate and not
  such a nag.
- I *should have* gotten off the couch and gotten
  a job. If only I had been a better spouse.

55

I want you to consider the possibility that you did the best you could, made the best choice in a spouse possible with the tools, history, information, and perspective you had at the time.

So you didn't listen to your gut and leave him when he admitted his sex addition.

You should have paid attention to the fact she flirted shamelessly with all of your friends.

So what, now what? Divorce is now your path, and being divorced is now your destiny. There is no benefit to beating yourself up because of your past choices. Simply put, self-flagellation does not serve you in any way. It only makes a bad situation worse, delays your healing, and make you feel awful. Doesn't it? And you're done with feeling awful, as we've discussed, yes? Yes.

Through therapy and/or coaching, you will find tools to expedite the process of self-forgiveness. Dare I say forgiving yourself is one of the first and most important steps toward the future you've begun to envision? Yes, I do dare to say that, because it is true. While you're searching for the right coach and best therapist for you, here's an exercise to get you started. Whip out your journal and answer these questions:

- What did I learn from my marriage about myself?
- What was great about my spouse and our marriage?
- What could I have done better?
- In what ways was I an awesome spouse?

If your journal isn't handy, no problem. Answer these questions in your mind, and be sure to jot them down later.

I'm sure you can admit your marriage wasn't all bad. You aren't a bad person, therefore you must be able to look back and find good things in your marriage, too. As a bonus, you can then presume that within you are the seeds of great things to come.

Feeling any better? Good, let's keep going.

I Have to Forgive My Ex? YES.

Of course, among the others who may need your forgiveness is your ex. In fact, next in the forgiveness line is your ex-spouse, even if you attribute the end of your marriage to his mother, her first ex-husband, or the person involved in an extra-marital affair.

You probably have some "if only's" and "should have's" for your spouse, too.

- *If only* she would have gotten help for her drug addiction.
- He *should have* told me he wanted more sex.
- *If only* she would have told me about her insecurities, instead of finding a boyfriend.
- He *should have* not let herself go.

I get it, and placing blame is the natural, and frankly human, thing to do. However, just as beating yourself up isn't productive, neither is blaming another person for how you feel or your circumstances.

I'm going to give you some tough love right now: *you chose your spouse*. If you had chosen a better spouse, you might still be happily married. Perhaps you ignored all of the signs that were there to see, because you were "in love." I get it. Been there, done that.

Own the fact that you chose in, and take 100% responsibility for that choice. See the marriage for what it was and what it wasn't, your spouse for who they were and weren't. Finally, forgive your spouse for their shortcomings, missteps, mistakes and overt indiscretions. Then, you'll be golden. Or at least on your way to golden.

Time for more action. Whip out your journal again and answer these questions:

- What did I learn about marriage from my spouse?
- What else was great about my spouse and our marriage that I didn't consider before today?
- What could my spouse have done better that I would like to see in a future relationship?
- In what ways was my spouse awesome?

What Forgiveness Is

I can hear you now, *"you want me to just let bygones be bygones, slap a smile on my face and get on with my day? You don't know my story, lady, and you just don't understand."*

Oh, but I do. I have my own story of cheating and abuse. Including some pretty awful legal battles, backstabbing you wouldn't believe, and horrible betrayal. But I chose my ex-husband and I put that original choice, and all of the results that followed, on me. I do that because then I'm not the victim, I'm the victor on my way to victory. By taking ownership of my situation, I release any belief I'm a victim at all. Because I control my thoughts, words and actions, I get to determine how I look at my ex and my marriage. So can you.

But let's look at this another way: holding a grudge is like drinking poison and wanting the other person to die. But that won't happen, your ex won't die because you think they should. Yet, you can die from "drinking too much poison," also known as, "the poison you are drinking when you expand the negative emotions you have about your ex when you talk or think about them in a way that makes you feel bad."

Forgiveness can be a gift that we give to ourselves.

Here are some of the easier steps towards forgiveness:

- Acknowledge your own inner pain. Yes, it happened. It sucks, really sucks. Speak it to your therapist, coach and/or inner circle, write it, feel it. The pain will eventually lessen and be gone.
- Express your emotions of anger, frustration and sadness in ways that don't hurt you or anyone else any further. You have every right to verbalize how you feel, as you work through your emotions, in a safe and empowering environment.
- Protect yourself from further victimization by limiting or eliminating, to the extent possible, contact with your ex-spouse.
- Try to understand the point of view and motivations of your ex-spouse; this will help you to replace anger with compassion.

- Actively forgive yourself for your role in the relationship. Using this mantra may help: *"I fully and freely forgive. I loose and let go. I let go and trust."*
- Perform the overt act of forgiveness verbally or in writing. If the person is dead or unreachable, you can still write down your feelings in a letter or your journal. Forgiving and moving on is one of the better ways to ensure your next relationship won't be the same or similar.

Forgiveness is "to give for one's self." Forgiveness, if you haven't made the connection yet, is about you!

What Forgiveness Isn't

Forgiveness isn't placing blame. It isn't pretending your marriage or the actions of yourself or your spouse didn't actually happen. It did happen, and it is important to retain the lessons learned without holding onto the pain.

Forgiveness is not excusing. We excuse a person who is not to blame. We forgive because a wrong was committed, and forgiveness is in our best interest.

Forgiveness is not giving permission to continue hurtful behaviors; nor is it condoning the behavior in the past or in the future.

Forgiveness is not reconciliation. We have to make a separate decision about whether to reconcile with the person we are forgiving or whether to maintain our distance.

Forgiving and letting go can be very difficult challenges, but it's even more toxic and stressful to hold on to grudges and hurt feelings. There are several symbolic letting-go rituals that can help with the process. If you are having trouble forgiving your ex, write him or her a letter expressing all of your feelings and explaining why you need to let go. You don't need to mail that letter, in fact it's better than you don't. It is cathartic enough just to write it all down. My minister, the late Dr. Arthur Caliandro, called it "the no stamps letter." The letter you write but never send, because it is in all reality, just for you.

You can also write down all of your thoughts, feelings, and emotions on a piece of paper and burn it, flush it, or cast it into the sea in a bottle when you are ready to really let go.

Are you ready to let go? I hope so, because letting go is going to feel amazing. I promise.

When Do I Have to Start Forgiving?

Umm, how about right now?

Forgiveness is free; you don't need to add it to your budget.

Forgiveness happens in an instant; you don't need to make time for it.

Forgiving those who have hurt you, up to and including yourself, feels (as I have already mentioned) so incredibly amazing.

The day I forgave myself and my ex-husband … and a few others, while I was at it … was such an amazing day. It happened in a therapy session. The therapist, incredibly skilled at calling me on my "stuff" showed me where I was pointing the finger at my ex, when I should have been pointing it squarely at myself. I needed to, she said, make a list of all of his great qualities, give him the latitude I would want him to extend to me, and get on with creating a new, different and better relationship. This was done in the context of co-parenting, and yet the person who arguably benefitted from the most from that transformation was actually me. I was even able to apologize for anything and everything he thought I did (real or imagined), and ask that we move forward in a positive way for the sake of our daughter.

Of course, my daughter benefits from our new-and-improved relationship as well, because she has parents who can and do communicate on a regular basis in a positive way.

If your union is ending without children, dare I say you don't have the increased emotion that comes from dealing with child support, visitation, and other issues of control that arise when parents separate. That is something for which you can be extremely grateful!

Regardless of your circumstances, forgiveness is the gift you give to yourself, for yourself. You deserve the gift, and you deserve it today. What are you waiting for?

I have found that people struggling with forgiveness can build on suggestions but have a hard time getting started. Try using a mantra or two to help you progress in your forgiveness.

If your ex cheated, was verbally abusive or had no drive, consider using these words of forgiveness as your mantra, inspired by Unity Minister Catherin Ponder: *I fully and freely forgive you. I loose you and let you go. I let go and trust.*

Divorce Stages

Depending upon where you are in your divorce process, you may be contending with more than just the "technical" aspects. In addition to finding an attorney, collecting documents, and divvying up assets, you are also dealing with the stages of divorce.

As with grief of any kind, it is common to move back and forth between the emotional stages of divorce – sometimes within a few minutes or hours! You may find some of the stages easier to navigate than others, depending upon whether you initiated the divorce or not. The thing to remember is that you eventually make your way through to the other side, feeling better and your new life.

The Emotional Stages of Divorce

Denial and Deliberation: You may find it hard to believe this is happening to you, especially if you were blind-sided by your spouse. You may initially refuse to accept the relationship is truly over and struggle with trying to find solutions to the marital problems. You will spend time believing that if you do or say the right thing your spouse, will come home and things will go back to normal. You hate feeling out of control about your destiny. You will be convinced that divorce is not the solution to the marital problems. Finally, you will have an encounter with your spouse, or discover something that will be the "last straw."

If you initiated the divorce, you will have moved through this stage even before your spouse was aware a divorce was happening. Don't be surprised as you watch your spouse contend with this stage.

Shock and Awe: You feel panic, relief, rage, liberation, and numbness, also know as, "Am I going completely crazy?!" You swing between despair that your marriage is over and hope that it will be restored. It seems impossible to cope with these feelings because honestly, they can be frustrating, overwhelming, overpowering and come in unexpected waves. You will experience some common fears when thinking about your future alone. You will wonder how you are going to survive your divorce. Will you ever find love again? Will the pain ever end? Will you feel this way forever? These are common questions and feelings in this stage, along with "I'm actually relieved. Is that odd?"

Rollercoaster and Transition: You can't seem to resolve your feelings and thoughts for any length of time. You feel great and hopeful one day, to feeling utter despair the next. During this stage, you try to intellectualize what has happened. If you can only understand what is going on, then the pain will go away and you will be able to make sense of everything. You tell yourself stories to try to make sense of it and your imagination will run wild. You wonder if there was more you could have done, or if there is anything wrong with you. Maybe your spouse never even loved you. You wonder if your entire marriage was a lie.

There is a lot of mental re-hashing during this period. You feel as if you can't control your thinking and find yourself obsessed with the failure of your marriage. Depression is a danger at this stage and you may cry at the drop of a hat or feel out of control. You and/or your spouse may engage in flings or affairs during this time, adding confusion and further complicating an already very complex situation.

Bargaining and Brokering: You could be holding on to hope that your marriage will be restored or doubting your decision to file. There is a willingness to change anything about yourself or thinking that if you could just get it right, your spouse would return. Or, you are contemplating doing things that will result in your spouse hating you so they will stop trying to win you back. The important thing to learn during this stage is that you can't control the thoughts, desires, or actions of any other human being.

Releasing and Letting Go: This is likely the stage you are in while reading this book, or trying really hard to get to: you realize the marriage is truly over, and there is nothing you can do or say to change this truth. You become more willing to forgive the faults of your ex and take responsibility for your part in the breakdown of the marriage. You begin to feel a sense of liberty and some hope for the future.

Acceptance: The obsessive thoughts have stopped, the need to heal yourself and put your marriage behind you. You begin to feel as if you can, you *will*, have a fulfilling life. Suddenly you are looking ahead to the life that awaits you, taking time to heal, making plans, and following through with them. This is a great stage! You open up to the idea of finding new interests, and move into a period of growth where you discover you have interests, strengths and talents you never knew existed! You are finally able to move forward in spite of the apprehension you feel. The pain gives way to hope and you discover that there is life after divorce and the future is made brighter due to the pain you have suffered.

Moving On:
Your Action Steps for Moving Forward

*Do whatever it takes to begin the forgiveness process: write your "no stamps" letter, answer the questions in this chapter, realize it's better to feel good than to hold onto resentment.

*Apologize for anything and everything you have ever done that could have hurt your ex. (Don't expect reciprocation. Just do it because you can.)

*Use a forgiveness mantra.

*Find yourself in the Emotional Stages of Divorce and know you are moving through them at the right pace and at the right time for you.

*Smile. You're still here, and you're doing great!

*"Put one foot in front of each other,
and eventually you will get where you want to go."*
~Honorée Corder

Chapter Four:
Rule #4: You Must Protect Yourself and Your Mental Health, Above All Else

"Self-care is not self-indulgence. It is the highest form of self-love and self-respect."
~Honorée Corder

Living in a marriage where your thoughts were dominated by another person's needs or wants, it is sometimes difficult to downshift into totally and completely thinking of just yourself and what you want and need.

If, during your marriage, you were under-appreciated, neglected, or worse, abused, your self-esteem has undoubtedly suffered as a result.

The end of your marriage can be the beginning of a new, more confident and self-assured you, and a new you starts with a few key behaviors, and some of them might also be new.

First and foremost, you must protect yourself and your mental health by putting an immediate stop to any contact you have with any person who was, or is, abusing you. This includes abusive in-person conversations, texts, calls, or emails. No contact, or contact limited to any children involved.

67

As you navigate the Emotional Stages of Divorce, you must begin to practice, or begin again the practice of self-care.

Self-Care is Supreme

Self-care is a touchy subject. That's because our society largely views self-care as selfish, indulgent, or sometimes even narcissistic.

Yet self-care is anything but self-indulgent, or selfish. Taking good care of yourself not only makes your life more fulfilling, but it also contributes to your well-being. During divorce, self-care can make the difference between just getting through the day and actually enjoying the day as it happens.

From years of personal experience, as well as from the work I've done in my executive coaching practice with many hardworking men and women, I've learned that when we care for ourselves consciously and with intention, we naturally begin to free ourselves to reach our highest potential and give our best selves to the world. The process of divorce can come as a shock, throwing us off of our equilibrium and bringing most, if not all, self-care to a screeching halt.

If self-care has never been on your agenda, the very fact that you are dealing with a divorce means there's no time like the present to include simple yet profound activities into your life that can make all of the difference to your mental, physical and spiritual health.

Make no mistake, self-care is not just for the fairer sex. Men will many times neglect themselves in favor of devoting themselves to their work, especially during the divorce process.

Here are three ways to incorporate self-care into your life during divorce:

1. Discover when, where, why, and how you feel deprived, unsafe, and unhappy.

First, it's important to figure out where you feel deprived of what are probably some much-needed things in your life. From there you will gain a good idea on how best to approach your self-care. Pull out your journal, and record the answers to these key questions:

- Where do I feel deprived?
- What do I need more of right now?
- What do I need less of?
- What do I want right now?
- What am I yearning for?
- Who or what is causing me to feel resentful and why?
- What am I starving for?

Be specific with your responses. You may recognize several areas that were neglected during your marriage such as time alone, physical touch, a neglected hobby, fun, or getting enough good sleep.

2. Identify your ideal routine.

Routine isn't boring. Rather, routine gives our lives stability, security, safety, and serenity. Routine is rejuvenating because it becomes part of who you are, and becomes something you can rely on thus reducing stress and increasing personal happiness. Getting enough sleep, exercise, volunteering, or having a girls' or guys' night out {GNOs} are all routines that restore and rejuvenate. To identify a routine that would matter, ask yourself, "What one activity could I put into place this month that would improve my life the most, that I could also do on a regular basis?"

Once identified, schedule that first appointment (such as a massage, facial, or haircut), and place a recurring appointment on your calendar. You should see the effects of your new activity after the first time, and after a few times, may recognize that you feel more relaxed, healthier, and less stressed.

3. Create an "absolutely *not* list."

Knowing what you *don't* want to do is just as important as knowing what you do want! In marriage, we sometimes will tolerate the actions or needs and desires of others in order to make or keep them happy, much to our own detriment. This list represents the things that you refuse to tolerate in your life, because they don't make you happy. Your ultimate goal is to create a list that makes you feel safe, protected, taken care of, and free to be your best self.

Some examples you may want to incorporate:

- Not rushing
- Not being late
- Not keeping anything that you don't love or need
- Not giving in to those people around you who are demanding or abusive
- Not answering the phone after 6 p.m.
- Not engaging in activities on one weekend day
- Not participating in gossip

Create your own list by looking for those activities you no longer do, no longer want to do, or would like to give up at some point in the future. If your spouse watched football every weekend during football season and it was never your thing, you never have to watch another game as long as you live. If your spouse made you watch the kids every Friday night so she could go party with her girlfriends, engage in something you want to do on those nights from now on.

Also, be sure to notice the things that frustrate you. For instance, maybe you're tired of attending meetings that aren't outcome focused. Use that for your list, and say this: "I only spend my time at work doing activities that serve me and my goals."

If you typically feel tension, tightness or aching, your body is telling you something. This might be a hint that you need to pay more attention to the activity you're engaging in that isn't exactly perfect for you.

Make a list of your new self-care best practices, post it in a visible place, and look at it every day. Mine is on my refrigerator, and just looking at it reduces my stress and reminds me I always have something to look forward to, such as my monthly massage, weekend walking workouts with my girlfriends, and a cup of tea and a new magazine a few times a month.

Extreme self-care takes practice. At first, it might seem awkward to say no to something or someone, and you might even feel guilty for taking time for yourself. But with practice, it will become more natural and automatic, and you'll notice that you feel a whole lot more fulfilled.

Put Yourself in "The Bubble"

The Boy in the Plastic Bubble is a 1976 made-for-TV movie inspired by the lives of David Vetter and Ted DeVita, who lacked effective immune systems. The film centers on the life of Tod Lubitch, who was born with an improperly functioning immune system. Contact with unfiltered air might kill him, so he must live out his life in incubator-like conditions. He lives with his parents, since they decided to move him from Texas Children's Hospital where he was being kept as a boy. He is constricted to staying in his room all his life, where he eats, learns, reads, and exercises, while being protected from the outside world by various coverings.

Just like Tod, you may be best served by living in "The Bubble," a place where you live, for a least a short time, in incubator-like circumstances. In your scenario, however, it isn't your immune system that is compromised, it is your self-esteem, self-worth, self-confidence, and self-image that needs ultimate protection, time to renew, and return to a normal state.

Your Bubble consists of some very simple rules:

Rule #1: You engage only in activities that make you feel great and are for your greatest good.

Rule #2: You surround yourself with people who lift you up, who you also lift up, and who are for your greatest good.

Seems simple, right? Simple, indeed! When you judge people and circumstances by those two rules, suddenly it is clear whether everything you do and everyone you meet is for your highest good and should be in your bubble ... or not.

And, of course, there's the concept of setting healthy boundaries.

Healthy Boundaries, People!

To maintain healthy boundaries, feel more centered and have the least amount of stress possible during your divorce, you must set healthy boundaries. Healthy for you, not anyone else. By virtue of the fact they are healthy for you, they will ultimately benefit your ex as well.

1. Check your personal engine light.

Think about how you feel when you're around your ex. Does she drain you and upset you? Is he someone with whom you feel you lose yourself? How does this feel in your body? How does it feel in your mind? How does the presence of this person affect you?

Now look at this list of feelings and sensations you've made, and imagine that your body is like a car, with a dashboard full of warning lights.

You've just identified what I like to call the "check engine light" for your personal boundary system. It's a security system warning that your personal energy field has been breached and you're letting in stuff that isn't yours.

This is really important. When our boundaries are weak, unguarded, or unclear, we let in all sorts of stuff that isn't actually our stuff, and we give away our own personal energy unconsciously.

That means you're dealing with a breach of your energetic security system and a leak of your own personal energy. You're looking at warning signs indicating that some work needs to be done, some boundaries need to be shored up, some self-care needs to be put in place, and you need to return to center.

Whether you're contemplating divorce, dead-center in the middle of your divorce, or ten years post-divorce, one can make the assumption there is or was a warning light or two that needs your undivided attention.

2. Ground yourself as preparation for maintaining boundaries.

Grounding is akin to the way a tree sinks its roots to stay secure in a storm. A tree with roots to the center of the earth is solid and unwavering, and that's how you want to be. Being grounded, especially during divorce, is your first tool in creating healthy boundaries; nurturing a connection with ourselves, and centering allows us to feel okay even in the midst of a storm.

Our root system is both our anchor and our boundary system. It keeps us from being blown about in other people's winds. It gives us a way to focus and still ourselves to connect with our heart and our intuition. That's what keeps us steady and connected and focused.

There are as many ways to get grounded as there are people. I like to take five minutes of solitude and silence to gain my center and imagine my root system connecting me into the earth, like a giant oak tree. Here are some other ideas:

- Meditation. I suggest Russell Simmons' book, *Success through Stillness*, for a simple yet incredibly effective and easy way to center. If you practice meditation daily, you'll be centered even before you need to be. My favorite meditation app is *Get Headspace*. You can use it for free for about 30 days, and once you're really into it, purchase access for a year of guided meditations.

- Saying a prayer, affirmation, or mantra in the shower in the morning, in the car on the way to work, or even while you're cooking dinner or working out. My suggested initial affirmation for you: *"All is well."*

- Offering a blessing over your meals or beverages.

- Chanting or repeating affirmations in your head as you do just about anything.

Try different ways, and soon you'll find the one that works for you. You'll know it's working because you'll feel the tension leave your body and a sense of calm and peace take over.

3. Notice the people and places that tend to drain you.

Before entering those places or exposing yourself to those people, take a few minutes to imagine breathing a bubble of protective energy around you. Think of it as a space that only allows love and positive energy inside, deflecting anything else. Really see it and really feel the force of it around you. Then, recognize what you need to do to maintain that space. If you know you're going to see your ex as you drop off the kids this weekend, make sure you're grounded and surrounded with great energy. Have somewhere to go immediately following, even if it's just to Starbucks for a chai tea or to meet the guys for a beer.

These three steps will help you create and maintain healthy boundaries. Building boundaries is like any muscle or practice: the more you work with it, and the better you get at it, and the better it serves you!

"No." It's a Complete Sentence

During the course of your marriage, you most likely accommodated your spouse and their needs and desires. If you have "nice person's disease," which I define as the desire to please others by saying "yes," "sure," or "absolutely" no matter who is asking, or when they're asking, or what they're asking, you may have found you put yourself in some pretty uncomfortable or undesirable situations. Much of the time, saying yes is to your detriment, both short and long-term. Now that you're divorcing, I have a tool you can use, and will want to use. In fact, the more you use it, the more you'll love it and want to use it.

The tool is this: Say no. In case you need it, let me give you special permission to say "no" (or one of it's close cousins "not yet" or "how about the 12th of never?"). The truth is, "No" is a complete sentence and requires no explanation whatsoever.

You are busy 24 hours a day, doing your best to get through your divorce, adapt to your new life, and take care of yourself. Taking on new projects and tasks is now a matter of sorting, prioritizing, and discarding. Sorting is the picking and choosing of the activities most important to you, and as you have a finite amount of time to do what needs to be done, you must look with a critical eye at each task prior to committing. Prioritizing is taking the chosen tasks and putting them in order of importance.

You must do these four things when a something or someone comes your way and is requesting your time and attention: (1) separate false urgency from real urgency using your current needs as the primary guide, (2) set expectations for saying yes based upon what you already have on your plate and the true urgency of the item, (3) let go of your need to please the person(s) asking and do what is best for you and your life, and (4) say "No" when necessary, politely and with a smile on your face.

It is absolutely fine to delay another person's desire for {instant} gratification and continue to stay focused on the most important person in the world right now: you.

Coach's Note: This is your life. Make it the way you want it. Keep in mind that you are the king or queen of your domain - you are far from being at the mercy of your ex, family, children, friends, boss, or clients.

Going "No Contact" with the Ex

As part of setting healthy boundaries, and depending upon the type of relationship you have with your ex today, it may be in your best interest to institute a "no contact" rule for a time or forever.

There are two ways a relationship ends: happily or with great sadness. Usually, one person is at least somewhat happy, and the other person is sad and heartbroken.

If you're the happy one, the no contact rule won't affect you that much, mostly because you're moving on and excited about it. However, if you're the one left heartbroken and miserable, then watching your ex post pictures on Facebook of his trip to Venice with his new girlfriend, or your wife having fun and looking hot as she has a girls' weekend in Napa, then going no contact is a definite must.

How to follow the no contact rule:

- Stop *talking*. If you have kids, institute an "in writing" contact system. You can email or text about the kids, their activities, weekly pick-up and drop-off, medical situations and school events. Let your ex know that if the email or text is hostile, sarcastic, abusive, or in any other way unproductive, you will not engage. As a last, although expensive resort, you can mandate all communication pass through your attorneys. Even the most narcissistic person won't want to spend $300 an hour to figure out visitation. No kids? Send all calls to voicemail, have someone you trust listen to their messages, and reply in writing.

- Still reading and still connected on Facebook? Stop right now and "unfriend" and block your ex. Let's face it, if you can be friends someday, it won't be for quite a while. Either because you're hurt, or because they are hurt. There are no two ways about it, you don't need to know what your ex is doing, how they are feeling, or who they are with ... for at least two years {and maybe never}.

- Stop anything and everything else you are doing to find out about your ex. Don't talk about him to mutual contacts, drive by his house, hack into his email, Google him, or … whatever else I didn't mention.

The Past, The Present & The Future: What's Your Vision

Regardless of how close to your Divorce Day you are today, if you don't have a clear, inspiring vision to cling to, there's never been a better day to start creating it.

I'm borrowing the following section on visioning from my book *Vision to Reality,* edited just for you.

Your Vision

Vision is what you see in your mind's eye, not something you see externally. You don't leave on vacation without knowing your destination, and this journey into your future is no different. The first step in creating a new life you love is the creating of your vision.

If you've never created a true vision before, it may seem like an exercise that is vague and intangible. The long-term benefits are absolutely beneficial and substantial and help you create results that can be simply amazing. Your vision, once crystalized, will literally pull you forward. It will get you up early, or even just get you up … and keep you up late. It will keep you excited, even when you do experience those inevitable post-divorce challenges, like when you get off-track, sick, or your progress is slower than you'd like. Indeed, your vision is the glue that holds this whole train together.

Your vision is your "what." When you close your eyes and think of what you truly want, you'll find that a picture of those desires appears on the mental screen of your mind. Even before you can formulate your vision, I encourage you to envision something much longer term, such as five or ten years. What's the longer-term vision you're working toward? Is it getting your kids off to college? Finally going back to school and getting the degree you've always wanted? Backpacking around Europe? Finding a new and wonderful person with whom you can spend many happy years? There's no right or wrong answer, the best answer is your honest answer. Write down five things you want to have accomplished five or ten years in the future.

If you're having trouble getting started, you may not be convinced of the power of creating a vision. In fact, you might be so stuck in your muck you can't imagine tomorrow, let alone the future.

All right, I'll take that as a challenge and do my best to convert you to a bona-fide enthusiastic long-term vision creator. Here are just a few reasons why visioning is something you should do:

- Visioning breaks you out of boundary thinking. As you open your mind and your mind's eye to new possibilities, you will begin to shed previous limitations.
- Visioning provides continuity and avoids the stutter effect of planning fits and starts. Having a defined, clear vision that is reviewed and visualized often – i.e., multiple times daily – will

help you avoid the "New Year's Eve Syndrome" ... where a vision is defined, only to be forgotten in about two weeks.

- Your vision automatically identifies your future direction and purpose. It grabs hold of your interest, strengthens your commitment, and promotes laser-like focus. When there is a clear picture in your mind of where you're going, it is always there, accessible and readily available to pull you in the right direction.

- Visioning encourages openness to unique and creative solutions. As you hold your clearly defined vision, the ways to make that vision happen become clear. Your subconscious mind works on your behalf to spot potential opportunities and possibilities you might otherwise have missed.

- Visioning promotes and builds confidence. Have you ever noticed how a person who has a purpose and a vision carries himself or herself in a certain way? They are positive, upbeat, and yes, confident. Your confidence is magnetic, attracting to you your clearly defined vision, and that very same vision can work magic for you. Becoming positive and magnetic might be who you used to be, or it might be who you've always wanted to be ... nevertheless, *positive, upbeat, and magnetic* are words you can someday soon use to describe yourself, with the right vision!

Are you convinced? You have already created in your life what you have previously held as a vision, even if you didn't realize that's what you were doing. The life you live now is the result of what was probably not a carefully crafted vision. Now is the time to use your subconscious mind through the use of this picturing tool to create what you truly desire, this time on purpose and with purpose. Think of vision as clear imagination, only this time you're using directed imagination and creating your future one magical moment at a time.

Your Visioning Exercise

Set aside some time to sit quietly, where you'll be undisturbed. You can get crazy and block off two hours, or you can close the door to your office or your bedroom for twenty minutes.

Start the process of creating your vision by daydreaming. Begin to imagine and create a colorful, clear picture in your mind what your life will look like when you feel amazing. When time, energy, people, space, and money are no object. What areas of your life are working really well? Do you have a new empowering relationship that is mutually beneficial, happy, healthy, even sexy? Imagine yourself as strong, fit, financially sound, balanced, fulfilled, and happy as you wish to be.

Keep asking yourself, "What is my preferred future?" and be sure to …

• Draw on your beliefs, mission, and mental picture of your model environment.
• Describe in detail what you want to see in the future.
• Be specific to each area of your life.
• Be positive and inspired.
• Be open to a massive upgrade, lots of changes, and a really big leap!

Here are some questions to get you started creating your vision:

- In your preferred future, what time does your day start? End? How many hours do you work or volunteer, and how is your day structured?
- Who is with you? It's no surprise our happiness is determined in large part by the people surrounding us, and it is time to become clear about whom you want to attract into your life in the future.
- What activities do you want included in your days, weeks, months, and years?
- What is your ideal living space? Where is it located? What do you drive?
- Where do you vacation? With whom? How often?
- Define your friends and other significant relationships.

Other thought-provoking and helpful questions:

- What will you gain from achieving your vision?
- What will the world gain from you achieving your vision?
- Who is going to help you?
- Who is going to help you enjoy the rewards?
- Where will you work on your vision?
- Where will you celebrate its achievement?
- When do you want to achieve different aspects of your vision?
- When are you going to start working on your vision?
- Why on earth are you going to dedicate your time, talents, and resources to work toward this vision?
- Why must you achieve your vision?
- Why are you worth your vision?

Brainstorm. Be specific. Be playful. Be creative. Make the vision of your life the way you want it. After all, it's your life and your vision!

Remember this: It is important to put your vision in writing. There is power in the written word. Just the act of writing down what you want sets the creative process in motion. Give yourself enough uninterrupted, focused time to go from start to finish of your first draft. If your initial visioning times have only lasted about twenty minutes, I recommend blocking two to three hours to complete the questions above. Then, let your vision sit for a while and come back to it after you've had time to reflect upon it. Your vision is alive; it is living and constantly-evolving. Keep in mind that what you think you want may actually not be what comes to fruition, but what comes to fruition may actually be way better!

Vision Killers

As you engage in the visioning process, you may encounter obstacles that also happen to be people. Just because you are on board with your new destiny doesn't mean everyone around you will or even can be. Be alert to the fact that you may encounter the following vision killers and be ready to ignore them.

Tradition: Be careful of the phrase "But it's always been done this way." Or, "You've always done it this way." Divorce allows for the intentional and deliberate evaluation of each area of our lives, visioning allows for the intentional and deliberate creation of our new life, including things we need to let go of or stop doing.

Fear of ridicule: Most often the people who criticize are those who have neglected to create their own vision and who come from a place of fear instead of power. Have compassion for them, but don't listen to them.

Stereotypes of people, conditions, roles, and outcomes: You may hear, "Why do you think you can achieve this?" Your answer: "Why not me?"

Naysayers: Very simply, refuse to listen to anyone who doesn't absolutely 100% support your vision. Period.

Look, some of these folks want to help you, warn you against doing something that could cause you to get hurt, or "lose everything." Most likely, they are coming from a good place and don't mean to inflict the harm that comes from sowing seeds of "you can't succeed." It's just that their advice and intention is run through their own filters, and those filters are often chock-full of limiting beliefs, past failures, and even frustration with their own lack of happiness in life.

Remember: there is no right or wrong way to write a vision! You should describe in full detail exactly what you desire. It may take up to 20 pages or more, or it may be as simple as one page of bullet points.

Moving On:
Your Action Steps for Moving Forward

*Begin the practice of self-care, *today.*

*Put yourself in "The Bubble" until you feel much better than you do today.

*Go "No Contact" with your ex, also *today.*

*Envision your vision. Pull out that journal and get to work!

"You deserve the best life has to offer, and today you're the person who can give it to you."
~Honorée Corder

Chapter Five:
Rule #5: You Must Not Make the Divorce About Money or Things

"Your joy and happiness is the most precious of your possessions." ~Honorée Corder

You First, Then Money, And Then Things

You can always make or manifest more money. You can always buy more things, I mean, there's a mall just down the street, right? But you cannot, *can not*, buy or find another <u>you</u> no matter how hard you look or how rich you are. You won't be able to get back the time you spent fighting over exactly how much you're getting in the divorce versus how much your ex is going to end up with, and you can always buy another antique marbled-topped table for your new entryway. Can't you?

Pam[†] was introduced to me by a trusted family lawyer. She was at the end of her divorce and stood to receive a hefty, million-dollar settlement and a nice monthly amount of child support for many years to come. Yet Pam was still focused on the past, angry at her ex for his gross transgressions, and particularly pissed off because he is a highly-compensated professional who stood to continue to make a hefty income, while she would have to make do on her settlement and child support.

[†] Not her real name.

He would continue to make money and be able to afford trips to Europe with his girlfriends, but those days were over for her. *He* would be able to buy the newest car, clothes and jewelry, while she would need to sell the house, downsize, and economize. *He* still would be able to live his life as if almost nothing had happened, but she would have to adjust to everything being new and different.

It took quite a few coaching sessions before Pam was able to make every conversation about herself, her life, and recognize that being focused on the future was in her best interest.

The divorce took an additional year and cost hundreds of thousands of dollars more than it should have, because she refused to take her ex's initial, reasonable offer – the amount she ended up settling for, only after countless trips to court over trivial items like the guest bedroom furniture, an old vehicle, and some china, hours on the phone with friends and family recounting every detail, as well as therapy several times a week to deal with the stress.

What is the Cost of the Argument?

The cost of an extensive legal battle over finances and possessions is not just money spent. While you will undoubtedly spend unnecessary dollars to argue over who gets what and how much, the true cost lies not in what you pay. The true and lasting cost is, in my humble opinion, what it costs you personally in your stress and overall mental and physical health.

You will spend a considerable amount of time and energy gathering documents, making your case, and documenting past activities. Is it truly worth it, or would you be better off going another direction?

The true question becomes, *"What is the cost to you of staying in the fight?"*

I'm not saying you should not exit your marriage with a fair settlement. Nor am I suggesting you walk away with nothing and rebuild from scratch.

I am suggesting there is another approach you can take that will preserve your mental and physical health, lower your stress level, and quite possibly give you a better outcome than a long, drawn-out fight ever could.

The facts are the facts, and in many states, equitable distribution is spelled out. The documentation provided, combined with your particular circumstances, stipulate the outcome. You, as a client, can instruct your attorney to act in your best interest, or you can choose to fight over items and assets. But, is continued litigation truly in your best interest? Would you not be better served to agree to a swift and somewhat equitable distribution of assets, rather than dig in your heels and continue to fight?

Only you can answer these questions, but I must point out something my corporate attorney told me of her experience as a litigation specialist:

> *"Many times people engage in litigation to get the attention of the other party. This attention is what they want and have been unable to get another way."*

Quite possibly you are the person who wants the attention of your ex, not the other way around. If this is you, *stop it*. Your marriage is over, the ship has sailed, and you are divorced or darn close to it. There's no sense in prolonging the inevitable. Give your attorney permission to negotiate a settlement in your best interest and let her do the back-and-forth. Your attorney will remain unemotionally involved while advocating on your behalf. This can all be done while you're busy growing your business, focusing on your kids, or even spending a week in Cabo with your girlfriends. In other words, while the details of your old life are being handled, you can begin to create your new life.

Repeat After Me: If You Want It, You Can Have It

When I was going through my divorce, which I will point out was not initiated by me, I was determined not to argue with my ex about anything. In fact, we were able to come to terms by ourselves about the division of money and assets.

Every so often, he would become concerned about something as though he was worried I was going to try to get away with something he really wanted. I decided early on I only really wanted two things: my businesses and primary physical custody of our daughter. Because we both had incomes, we amicably agreed to the distribution of our savings and investments. When it came time to talk about our "stuff," I gave him first right of refusal, always using this statement:

"If you want it, you can have it. If you don't want it, I'd like the option to have it. But if you want it, you can have it."

90

In other words, don't take everything and burn it or donate it to Goodwill just to be spiteful. Take what you want and let me have the option to take anything you don't really want.

This stance worked beautifully, because it caused him to make sure I got what I needed, too. We had purchased beautiful living room furniture not quite a year before our split. While he could have had the whole set, because I was unattached and kept my focus on what I *really* wanted {and it certainly wasn't to make sure I had *that couch* or *this particular lamp}*, I let him pick the items he wanted. Out of fairness and a sense of reciprocity, he made sure my daughter and I had a couch.

Play Win-Win {-Win}

What was interesting about being unattached and willing to let my ex have what he wanted was how much less stress I felt. Becoming a single mom can be enough to drive a person mad, and I didn't have the added stress of a high-conflict divorce to add to my plate.

About a decade before my divorce began, I had read *The 7 Habits of Highly Effective People*. Habit 4 is "Think Win-Win." As Stephen Covey points out in this epic bestseller, *"Think Win-Win isn't about being nice, nor is it a quick-fix technique. It is a character-based code for human interaction and collaboration."*

Your divorce isn't a competition to see who can get more, move on to a new romance faster, or get the most love from the kids.

Your divorce is an opportunity to graciously, and for the good of all concerned, end a relationship and life together that did not work in order to begin a new and happier life.

Playing win-win isn't necessarily fun or easy, but it is good for you {win}, good for your ex {win} and good for your children {bonus win}. Win-win-win.

In case you're all in for the win-win-win, but you're not quite sure what to do, here are your guidelines:

- Act with integrity. Tell the truth. Be forthcoming. Be fair. Keep your negative opinions and observations to yourself. Said another way, don't say or do something you wouldn't want written about on the cover of *The New York Times*.

- Keep your side of the street clean. It doesn't matter what your ex does to try to spin you up or get your goat or piss you off or frustrate you or make you sad, don't have any of it. Ignore bad behavior, reward good behavior. Said another way, don't do anything you're going to have to apologize for later, or something you would regret admitting you had done.

- Do the right thing because it's the right thing to do. Enough said.

Be Willing to Let It All Go to Start Over

In the event your ex has not read this book and is not taking your new enlightened view of a better, happier and easier divorce, you may be best served by cutting your losses and walking away. Continuing to fight could mean you'll end up with more money. It could mean you'll end up with your grandmother's hand-carved antique clock with the gold inlay. But it could also mean you run the risk of suffering serious health consequences, maxing out on stress, anxiety, or worse.

If it looks like your ex wants to fight to get your attention for the foreseeable future, consult your attorney about what it would take to give an uncontested divorce in which she gets everything she wants, except you. You're going to need you, and you can always make or manifest more money, more furniture, more important personal possessions. You've made it this far, right?

You're going to come out of your divorce with you fully intact, and you are all you need, baby! You've got this!

Moving On:
Your Action Steps for Moving Forward

*Envision your vision.
*Let go and get moving!
*Play "win-win."

"Take a deep breath, fill up with peace, and know everything is going to be alright."
~Honorée Corder

Chapter Six:
Rule #6: You Can't Move Forward Until You've Signed the Papers

"Your divorce is really over when it's really over."
~Honorée Corder

If you think the day you or your ex moved into separate quarters is when your new life began, it's time for a quick dose of reality. Just as you weren't married until you walked down the aisle and said, "I do," you're not truly divorced until you're actually divorced. Your new life technically doesn't truly begin until you receive your divorce decree.

It's Not a Divorce Until There's a Judgment

What's the real difference between being separated and actually divorced? Again, just like with marriage, it's not all about the piece of paper. The piece of paper does, however, have a huge psychological impact. Unless and until you've actually received your final judgment for divorce, you won't know exactly what I'm talking about.

Your decree will most likely arrive in a plain brown envelope, and what happens emotionally when you read, in ubiquitous language, a summary of and the terms of your divorce can bring you to your knees. The document shouldn't be shocking, and yet it may be. You might not think you will be overwhelmed with emotion, and yet you may be. Once you've received your decree, you will be faced with working your way through the emotional stages that come with a divorce. And, as we've discussed, they are very similar to those we experience at the death of a loved one.

Reasonable Self-Expectations

Because the emotions of divorce can be overwhelming and expected and unexpected at the very same time, it is prudent to be gentle with yourself and set reasonable expectations. Don't be surprised if you want to lash out, take a long nap, or feel like overeating. You might even feel like having a very large party. Behaviors that lean on the excessive side are normal, almost expected, as you navigate divorce.

On the scale of the Holmes and Rahe Stress Scale, divorce ranks second only behind the death of a spouse, above moving, jail, the death of a family member, and even getting fired.

You may think "I've got this" only to find there are times when you know for sure you definitely don't have it.

Cut yourself some slack. If the goals you've set aren't coming to fruition as quickly as you'd like, allow yourself to be okay with slower timing. Give yourself some leeway if your home isn't as neat as you feel it should be, or if you've gained or lost some weight in the process. Don't expect life to be normal right now. As a matter of fact, expect life to be the opposite of normal for a while. Now is the time to be especially gentle with yourself, go with the flow, take everything a little less seriously, lower your expectations about, well, just about everything, and take life one day at a time.

What's Your Runway?

By runway, I mean "how long will it be before you feel like yourself again." The time honestly depends on you, your attitude, and your expectations. The amount of time you'll spend *on the ground* after divorce is largely connected to your mental make-up in general, i.e., are you generally a positive or negative thinker? Before your divorce, did you wake up each day with a sense of positive expectation or a sense of dread? Do you generally think the world is a great place full of great people or a lousy place full of lousy people?

Your basic belief system will play not only into your divorce experience, but your post-divorce experience as well.

The divorce may have skewed your basic settings as well. If before the divorce you felt you were a positive person in a great marriage, only to find out your spouse started cheating on you shortly after you were married, left you thousands of dollars in debt, and was secretly a serial killer, you may find you look at the world through a slightly darker lens. However, on days you feel fully liberated post-divorce, you might just be wearing rose colored glasses.

By all means, take the actions that are necessary right now, such as changing your name, updating your insurance policies, removing names from bank and credit card accounts. By the same token, right now you must delay major decisions. Don't jump right into another relationship, or get into debt.

Two Years?!?

My therapist gave me the grave news, post-separation and pre-divorce, that it would take me two years to heal from my marriage and be ready to take on a new relationship.

This was me: *"Oh, but I'm unique and special. I should be good-as-new and back in the saddle in no time at all."*

Oh, how I wish I was right and she was wrong. But, alas, she and therapists around the world agree that the two year rule applies: working your way through the emotional stages of divorce and healing your broken heart takes about two years. They agree you should wait to begin a new relationship for at least two years, delay all major decisions during that time and focus on you and your healing.

I wish I had better news, I would love to tell you that on Friday afternoon you can finalize your divorce and by Saturday night be healthily involved in a new romance, but alas, I would be lying to you. I'm pretty sure you don't want to be lied to, and I don't want to lie, so we are where we are.

Waiting two years to start a new romance doesn't mean you're dead, or that you don't want or need companionship. The waiting allows the healing to take place so that when you do begin a new romance, you can do so without the thumps and bumps that can occur when our past encroaches on our future. If you have unresolved sadness, anger, or hurt that contributes to lack of trust, you won't be able to give yourself fully to a new person, no matter how fantastic they truly are. You wouldn't want to mess something up with a new and wonderful partner because you hadn't closed the loop on your marriage would you? I know you wouldn't!

Your New Day One

The day your divorce decree arrives is your new Day One. If you've already had it, and didn't know it, you get to declare today or any day in the future your new Day One. If you haven't yet received the decree, you have something to look forward to.

If you're working with a divorce coach or contemplating working with one, together you can create a plan for the next 30 or 100 days, also known as the first 30 or 100 days of your new life. Much like a newborn baby or the survivor of a traumatic accident, you will be learning things after Day One and feel as though you're learning them for the first time. The learning curve of life after divorce can be steep and tumultuous. Having a plan and positive activities and goals to focus on can remove some of the sting that accompanies that plain brown envelope.

Moving On:
Your Action Steps for Moving Forward

*Set reasonable self-expectations, and be patient with yourself as you move forward.
*Embrace your new Day One.
*Give yourself the full two years. Circle the date on your paper calendar or set a reminder in your online calendar. It will be here soon enough!

"Your Day One is the beginning of a new and wonderful life. Smile!" ~Honorée Corder

Chapter Seven:
Rule #7: You Must Nurture Yourself to Thrive

"The past is behind you. The future is meant to be designed by you. Enjoy today, as it truly is a present." ~Honorée Corder

Since page one, my goal for you is to give you back any power you feel you may have lost during your marriage, or have never had at all. I believe all power comes through self-esteem and self-awareness.

Just as you began to define what ideal self-care looks like for you, you can also begin to evaluate your physical, mental, and spiritual needs, also known as your Personal Needs, as a newly-divorced person. If your wife hasn't touched you since the Reagan era, or your husband gave you back-handed compliments instead of genuine words of affirmation, you probably have a Personal Need deficiency and will benefit greatly from spending some time with yourself discovering more about yourself and what you need.

Identifying Your Personal Needs

Each person has a unique set of Personal Needs (above basic survival needs) that must be met in order to be at their best. Meeting these needs are critical in order to thrive. As important as Personal Needs are, few people are aware of them, and as a result, they generally go about meeting their needs unconsciously, often in ways that are at odds with living a fulfilling life. Said another way, if you don't get your Personal Needs met in a positive way, you will get them met in any way possible and most likely, in a negative way. Post-divorce, the chances of engaging in negative activities in an attempt to fulfill our Personal Needs is very high. It is important for you to spend time discovering your Personal Needs and how to meet them in positive, constructive ways that work, and as you do, your life will tend to work. And, understanding your personal needs will help your life keep getting better and better ... and the bonus side benefit is you will become a more effective decision maker.

Characteristics of Personal Needs:

- They are critical for you to thrive and live a life you love;
- They are neither good nor bad; and
- They can be met in positive or negative ways relative to your desired results.

Think of Personal Needs as the underlying experience, or feeling, you are attempting to create through your actions.

Some examples of Personal Needs include:

- Acceptance
- Accomplishment
- Adventure
- Autonomy
- Challenge
- Connection
- Contribution
- Control

102

- Creativity
- Discovery
- Drama
- Excitement
- Freedom
- Harmony
- Importance
- Independence
- Influence
- Intellect
- Intensity
- Intimacy
- Power
- Recognition
- Simplicity
- Safety

This list is by no means exhaustive; it is intended to provide examples that will be a starting point for you and will be helpful to you in identifying similar (or different) words that accurately describe your Personal Needs.

3 Steps to Identifying Your Personal Needs:

1. Discover the possibilities. This step is about identifying all of the possible Personal Needs that you might have. Pull out your journal and write down:

- things in your life that bring you the most joy
- times in your life you have felt most successful
- times in your life you have felt least successful
- patterns you repeat that do not create the results that you want; identify the experiences you generate through these patterns and how you could generate them in more positive ways.

2) Refine your list. This process is designed to help you narrow your list so that it includes only those Personal Needs that are most important to you.

- Identify the eight to ten experiences that appear most often
- Consider which are *needs* (i.e. must haves) versus wants, shoulds, wishes
- Carefully consider those that you have a strong aversion to. Could they be needs that you don't like/want to take ownership of? If they are showing up as negative patterns, they might actually be important Personal Needs.
- Select the four Personal Needs that you determine to be most important to you.

3) Create a Plan. The idea here is that you want to be satisfying your Personal Needs automatically at all times, so that they are handled once and for all. Trust me, it is SO cool to be in a space where your needs are automatically met!

- Make a list of activities/actions that will help you meet your Personal Needs in beneficial ways; include the things you do every day as well as periodic activities and new things you could do to meet your needs
- Make a list of characteristics and behaviors that help you meet your Personal Needs
- Write down ways that other people can help you meet your Personal Needs and include them as determined by you

Positive Ways to Meet Your Needs:

In order to thrive, it is important to meet your Personal Needs in positive ways that enhance your enjoyment of life and/or the quality of your relationships. Examples of positive ways to meet your needs:

- Learning a new skill
- Taking more "me" time and engaging in extreme self-care
- Developing strong and healthy relationships
- Working smarter, not harder
- Expressing your feelings in a constructive way
- Writing a book
- Volunteer work
- Playing team sports
- Going on an adventure
- Getting regular massages, facials, or any other pampering that makes you happy.

Whether you are conscious of it or not, you have spent much of your life attempting to meet your Personal Needs. We do everything in our lives in the quest for experiences; the experiences that are most important to us are our Personal Needs. The more you know about yourself and what is important to you, the more likely you will be to choose positive ways to meet your needs so that you get what you really want.

Awareness of your Personal Needs is the first step toward meeting them in ways that are positive, which contributes greatly to the likelihood that you will thrive and live a life you love.

Thriving, Not Surviving

By now you've probably figured out that I don't believe your divorce is the end of you. In fact, I bet you've identified me as a card-carrying optimist. If that's the case, you are 100% correct. I don't think you should just survive your divorce, barely making it through the day and "coping." No, sir, I believe that as you shed the old relationship that clearly no longer serves you, it is time for you to step into your greatness and truly design a life that thrills you. It could even be time, dare I say, for you to find your passion and live your purpose for being on this planet. Sometimes in marriage, we truly do lose ourselves, push away our hopes, and deny our dreams in favor of pleasing a spouse and raising our children.

I want you to know that your divorce could be one of the very best things that ever happens to you. And I know you may have read the previous sentence more than one time. As I was facing divorce, and being a single mom, I thought life was o-v-e-r. I thought my relationship choices had left me doomed for life, and I would never have the chance to be truly happy.

How wrong I was!

Today I am happily remarried for a half-dozen years. I have two thriving businesses and I wake up pretty darn happy almost every single day, living my dreams and learning and growing.

If you, or anyone else, had told me that a dozen years after my divorce my life would even remotely resemble what it does today, I would have had you committed!

Please do the best you can to release your fears and anxieties and begin to move forward as soon as you can.

Make the List that Makes You Happy

Happy by Pharrell Williams is currently my favorite song *and* my ringtone. Even if I'm not thrilled to see who is calling, I'm delighted for the call so I can hear that song. It just makes me happy every time I hear it.

If you don't currently have a list of things that make you happy, pull out your journal one more time and begin to make a list. It can be simple things like "a hug from my daughter" (that's on my list for sure), or "getting a hand-written card in the mail" (also on my list) to bigger things like "buying a new car" or "taking a trip to Europe." If you're newly divorced and along with that, newly poor, don't get upset about that fact that you can't jet off to Paris on a moment's notice or that your car is ten years old. I will tell you something that will probably make a lot of sense to you: the best things in life really are free.

Case in point: right now, my daughter stands just a few inches shorter than me. In fact, when she hugs me, her head tucks very nicely under my chin. Hugging her is one of my favorite things to do, and I know in a few years, I will have to wait days, weeks, or even months for those hugs as she goes and lives her own life. My cat, Mr. Sylvester Pickles, runs to me when I come home no matter how long I've been gone (even if I just go and check the mail). My girlfriend Vanessa and I go for a walk every weekend to catch up and get in our 10,000 steps before it gets too hot outside. My COO, bestie, and shoe-shopping buddy Joan and I have the best time during our bi-annual retreats. We hole up at a hotel, plan our companies' futures, and spend a lot of time laughing.

I know for a fact that when I am tired, hungry, stressed, or sick, I'm not my most resourceful self. I would guess the same about you, and we can add "going through a divorce" to that list. You may just not be at your most resourceful, and either stuck or spinning your wheels, desperately wanting to feel better and yet not knowing what to do.

Take out your journal and create a list of the people, things and activities (positive, please!) guaranteed to put a smile on your face. Next to each person, write his or her phone number. Pull out your calendar and schedule a few activities with each of them. If you can, buy something on your list that makes you happy.

Tear out or separately create the list in your computer and print it out and put it on your refrigerator. If the list needs to remain private, tape it to the inside of your medicine cabinet door or the back of your master closet door. As we know emotion is created by motion, the next time you're feeling sad or hopeless, run to that list and either call someone on the list or do something on the list. For the first year after my divorce, I had a list of friends I could call at all hours, and a list of things I loved to do that were within my budget (like going to the bookstore for chai tea and reading a weekly magazine) hanging on my fridge. When you're not feeling good, you're just a couple of choices away from making a shift and getting to a better place.

What Isn't Nurturing {and I Mean It!}

Up to this point I've glossed over "negative activities" and I would be remiss if I didn't address, head on, some of the less-than-awesome things I've heard about and witnessed first-hand in folks going through divorce.

The three biggest unhealthy behaviors are: drugs, drinking, and sex. There is nothing wrong with social drinking, and sex is a natural activity every human being needs. However! When alcohol, drugs or sex are used as an escape or coping mechanism, they can be the beginning of a much bigger problem, one that needs to be addressed and healed.

Jerry was married to his elementary school sweetheart, Emily, for twenty-two years when she finally tired of his carousing and drug and alcohol addiction. A functioning alcoholic and occasional drug user, he ran a successful financial advisory business he and Emily had built from the ground up. Blind-sided in many ways by the divorce, Jerry, also a father of three small children, sought refuge in casual sex and copious amounts of drugs and alcohol. This caused him to lose several large clients, most of his net worth, and the respect of his friends and colleagues. It also destroyed his relationship with his ex-wife, and he missed most scheduled visits with his kids. As a somewhat public figure in his community, people started to notice that the man they thought they knew was engaging in questionable behaviors, and his reputation took a large hit.

Although he has since gotten clean and sober and is in the process of rebuilding his business and personal relationships, Jerry lost the respect of friends and colleagues alike. While a few have stood by him, others are waiting for the other shoe to drop while keeping their distance.

I share this as a cautionary tale of what can happen as one moves through the divorce process. If you are using or abusing drugs, drinking more than a drink or two a day, and engaging in promiscuous sex, I'm not your mother and not here to chide you. I'm going to suggest these actions are a symptom of a bigger hurt, a hole you're trying to fill, and perhaps you may want to seek help so you don't suffer long-term consequences for short-term choices.

Moving On:
Your Action Steps for Moving Forward

*Identify your four most important Personal Needs and create a plan to get them met!
*Make your Happy List
*Create your list of the people who make you happy and put their names and numbers on your fridge

"Happiness is an action that starts with you."
~Honorée Corder

Chapter Eight:
Rule #8: You Will Find Love Again, If and When You Want To

"You can find love again. There is evidence of this truth everywhere. You just must look for it and be open to it." ~Honorée Corder

"It's time. I'm ready!"

Have you said these words to yourself, specifically about getting back "on the market?" After divorce, it may seem an impossible task to get back into the dating scene.

Maybe what you've said is "No thanks! I've had enough of relationships."

I can identify with this sentiment, too. I couldn't seem to find a decent, honorable, and/or faithful man anywhere, so after a few years of unsuccessful and stressful dating, I took a break. That break lasted more than three years.

You Don't Have to Be With Someone

It is perfectly fine, thank you very much, to spend as much time being single as you want. Nothing says you need to be coupled up lickety-split. Being single has many advantages, and there is certainly no reason to rush. *However,* if and when you are ready, there are plenty of amazingly cool people in the world and there are probably a few hundred that could be a good match for you. You just have to go and find them!

111

What Works in Love After Divorce

I didn't seek dating advice from any known love and relationship experts after my separation and divorce. My initial confidants were arm-chair therapists, divorced themselves, who had navigated the divorce and dating process and had their own thoughts on what I could and should do next.

As I wrote in *The Successful Single Mom,* before I was divorced, I went to see a therapist immediately to seek help with my marriage. When my ex wouldn't participate, that therapy turned into a process to help me heal my childhood wounds, understand why I chose the husband I chose, and navigate the trauma of divorce and life after divorce.

While I'm not a therapist, matchmaker, or even expert on human behavior, I am a student of human behavior and *what works.* It seemed to me that if I could figure out how to run a computer program, learn a language, teach myself sales and marketing skills and procedures, and identify personality types, that I could read or listen to the relationship experts and figure out how to find the perfect mate for me.

I knew from therapy that I needed to work on myself and spend some time healing before I could be emotionally available to someone else. Logically, I knew that my daughter, business, and I needed all of my energy. Emotionally, I wanted someone to love me, cheer me on, support my dreams and goals, and be a partner in raising my daughter.

A tall order, for sure! I wanted the formula, the path, or the method that would have all of those wants fall into place easily and effortlessly. I think that's human nature, to want the path of least resistance. I did find what worked for me, and it only took about a million times longer than I wanted it to. It will probably take longer than you want it to take.

Because I've now been happily married for almost six years to a wonderful man (by anyone's standards), the question I get most often from my divorced friends is: "How did you find him?"

Well, I'll tell you. After making *all* of the most common dating mistakes people make, I decided to be completely single so I could work on myself. I clearly wasn't attracting the type of person I said I wanted. The common denominator in my lack-of-love life was, unfortunately, *me*. In conjunction with this break from the opposite sex, I began to read, listen to, and study the advice of the experts.

I learned that the challenges I was facing were common to many others. I learned how our biology dictates what we do, when we do it, and how we do it. I also learned that my personal biology, designed for the cave woman I wasn't; the cave woman who was unable to speak, yet demanded I make certain moves, wasn't doing me any favors. I also uncovered how to develop the courage to identify and speak the truth about what I wanted and didn't want in a partner and to *speak that truth to the men I was dating even before I started dating them.* A counter-intuitive concept, for sure, but one that really works.

Are You Really Ready?

I believe you are truly ready to begin the search for a new, amazing, and mutually-beneficial relationship when a few boxes have been checked:

- You are truly, absolutely, 100% single.
- You've been single for at least two years.
- You are emotionally neutral about your ex. Being neutral will require some work on your part, which we have discussed in detail in previous chapters.
- You are willing to commit to the process of finding the person who is perfect for you, no matter how long it takes, and not settling for less than you deserve in the meantime.

For the record, single is defined as "divorce decree received."

Until you've received the actual divorce decree, the scars left behind by the trauma of being in a relationship that didn't work as planned, can and will inhibit your ability to love yourself and to trust and love someone else fully.

Think of finding a new love in this way: it is impossible to buy a new wardrobe, bring it home, and put it in a closet that's already full. You must first get rid of what you do not want in order to make room for what you do want. So, as long as your ex occupies the important real-estate contained in your heart and mind, it won't be possible for an authentic new love to blossom fully.

Clean Out Your Heart to Fill It Up Again

I have talked a lot about forgiveness and working through any unresolved emotions with regard to your ex. It is no joke, and I am not kidding: when I say you must get to a place of true emotional neutrality regarding your ex-spouse before you can be truly in a place to move forward romantically, I'm completely serious.

Don't think you can sweep your feelings under the rug and move into a new situation without those emotions coming from out of nowhere and knocking you right on your keister at the most inopportune moment.

Only you know where you truly are at this moment, and whether you need a therapist, a divorce coach, or both. Be honest with yourself by doing a self-inventory and getting clear on you. If you get the help you need, I promise you the personal development you do will pay dividends for the rest of your life.

Falling In Love With You

I believe the most attractive quality in any person is *self-confidence with the second being authenticity.* Part of being self-confident and authentic is knowing and loving yourself fully, unabashedly, and unapologetically. Finding a new love relationship begins with feeling great about yourself – literally falling in love with you!

You are most attractive to others when you are most attractive to yourself. When you can look in the mirror and say, "Damn, I look *good* today!" you will walk out the door and find that others react to you in a positive way.

If you don't feel that way now (yet), the world is losing out and so are you. The one thing you have in your power is what you are doing to make yourself feel amazing. If you are not emotionally feeling great, it is very easy not to make the effort to look great.

Keep in mind you deserve to look great and feel great, physically, and emotionally.

Last week, I was most definitely not feeling great. I was under the weather. I just wanted to wear all black, preferably pajamas, and stay on the couch all day. I put on all black, but threw on a camel jacket and a fun leopard-print hat and went out to a meeting anyway. I got a dozen compliments (ten of them about how much they liked the hat), and by the time I was on my way home, I literally felt so much better. Trust me, I don't always want to rally, get all gussied up, and face people; however, I do it anyway, and every single time, I'm glad I did.

Take the time to pull yourself together and look nice. You don't have to be dressed to attend a gala, just good enough that you feel great and if you happened to run into your ex, you wouldn't be embarrassed and kicking yourself for not putting on something a little nicer. When you look good, you feel good (or at least a little better than before), and the extra effort is worth the time it takes.

I think exercise, diet, rest, meditation, attitude, time with friends, and a spiritual connection are the other critical elements that factor into our self-love. In turn, this self-love radiates outward to the world as self-confidence and authenticity.

Exercise

If, like me, your relationship ended, and you found yourself with some extra pounds, now is the perfect time to add some exercise into your routine. I work out less than thirty minutes per day, and I'm addicted to those endorphins, not to mention the fact that my

116

pants still fit. You'll be hard-pressed to find folks who added regular exercise into their life and aren't happy about it.

When all else fails, you can go for an after-dinner walk or incorporate yoga into your morning. I do my best to hit the mat a couple of times a week, and I feel like it truly makes a difference. Whatever you do, do something because it will help you to feel better immediately following your exercise and during the rest of your day as well.

Diet

What you eat, and don't eat, makes a major difference in how you feel. If your diet consists of foods that don't feed your body effectively, you're going to feel and see the difference. When you eat healthy intentionally, drink more water, and watch your portion sizes, you will have more energy, see your weight settle at a natural place, and even sleep better.

Rest

Without enough sleep, I'm wearing my cranky pants. There's no doubt about that! I need at least 7-8 hours of sleep a night, and without it, I'm simply not at my best. When I go to bed "on time," I actually wake up before my 5 a.m. alarm and have enough stamina and energy to handle whatever comes in my direction throughout the day.

Meditation

As I've previously mentioned, meditation is my secret weapon for managing the stress of being a wife and mom, owning businesses, and life in general. I discovered The Silva Method in my early 20s, and within that method is an amazing 26-minute meditation that I do almost every day (and twice in a row on days when I don't get enough sleep). Each relaxation cycle is equal to three to four hours of sleep. If you're like me, turning off your brain for even five minutes is virtually impossible! I use guided meditations, and they work wonders. Even though it took me quite a while to be able to just listen to the meditation, relax, and not allow my monkey mind to take over, it was worth sticking with it. Meditation is definitely a gift you should look into giving yourself!

Attitude

A big part of being magnetically attractive to oneself as well as the opposite sex is having a positive mental attitude. I would be remiss if I didn't share my tried-and-true method for getting and keeping an attitude that serves you.

If I had to choose one key component for achieving the highest possible levels of success for an individual, it's attitude all the way. Having a rock-solid, fantastic attitude is not just necessary, it is crucial. Long before anyone knows whether you've got the skills, they feel your sizzle ... or your lack of it!

As you're navigating the daily challenges of adjusting to dating in today's world along with being single in general, it is easy to lose hold of your outlook, feel overwhelmed, and become frustrated. Here are some of the most effective beliefs to adopt *right away* that will allow you to get – and keep – an attitude that's going to help make your life just this side of painless.

"I learn from everything." The questions we ask ourselves can make or break us. When challenges hit, and they do, one power question to pose right away is: "What is the lesson for me in this situation?" Have you noticed when you don't learn your lesson the first time, you end up in the same or similar, and many times more painful, situation again? By asking that question, you can nail down what you're supposed to learn from the situation in order to avoid repeating it in the future.

The second part of this learning process is putting systems in place so the lesson will automatically not repeat itself. The next question is, "What are ten ways I can make sure this situation never happens again?" This list is a brain-storming session that enables you to learn from the fresh wound and avoid future ones.

Here's an example that might help: You get in your car just in time to get to work, and you'll arrive for your first scheduled meeting if you leave now. As you turn the ignition, you notice the "low fuel" light is on. Rats! Now you have to take at least five minutes to gas up, leaving the possibility wide-open that you will be late. I used to experience this quite a bit. Now I have my car cleaned and gassed up at least once a week, and more often if I notice the gauge falls below the half-tank marker. That way, I never have to stop when I should be on my way. Spend time identifying and addressing your "gaps" early will allow you to safeguard yourself and prevent future hardship.

Each time you experience a challenge, spend time later thinking about how you can prevent it in the future and document what you discover in your journal.

"This too shall pass." Remember this: You feel the worst when you're in the midst of the crisis, and a divorce is nothing if not a crisis. It is easy to lose perspective and give up hope. This is the best time to stay steadfast in your conviction. Keep your vision, goals, and dreams vividly in your mind. Life consists of seasons, as do situations. There will come a day when the awful problem you're having now will be a distant memory. Prepare to triumph over this situation now by remembering "This too shall pass."

"No retreat, no surrender!" This mindset is critical for you to adopt, preferably sooner rather than later and hopefully when you're not already in the midst of a crisis. Do not back down from adversity.

Use this as your mantra repeatedly: *"I have it in me to face and overcome anything that comes my way."* Repeat as often as needed or even if it is not needed.

If you're not entirely convinced this mantra is true, think back to other times when you thought the world was coming to an end. If you're reading this book, you're still here! Even if you've only been in the divorce process for all of ten minutes, you have gotten this far, and what has brought you here is a strong foundation for getting you where you want to end up.

Evaluate how you will choose to move forward, keeping in mind that one super-effective choice available to you includes "bend but don't break." Think of trees in a storm. They gracefully accommodate natural forces while staying strongly anchored by their foundation. Think of yourself as a tree in the face of your storms and sway in the face of difficulty without giving in.

"It's half-full *not* half-empty!" Most people possess a dual thought process: "I'm awesome; well, maybe not so much." A tennis match seems to be going on in their heads, an argument of will that in one moment serves them in their quest to move forward and the next takes the wind out of their sails. Seeing the glass as half-full really isn't the Pollyanna approach; instead, it's the approach that allows you to retain hope. Hope is the single, most named factor when people are polled about how they survived and even thrived in the face of adversity. Keep hope alive, and you're keeping your dreams alive and increasing your chances of goal achievement!

"If it's to be, it's up to me." The only person who can make "it" (whatever you want) happen is you. The only thing or person standing in the way of your own success, love, and happiness is you. By adopting this attitude, you set in motion invisible forces that will come to your aid. You also raise your vibration and will attract to you what you need to achieve your every desire. Staying in "possibility thinking" will keep you focused on how you can accomplish **anything you want**. If you're going to argue for something, argue for how you can make it happen, instead of arguing about how it is just not going to happen.

As you can see, simple shifts in your personal attitude will make all the difference. You will feel better, which means you will be more resourceful about everything, not just in choosing your new love.

Girls' & Guys' Night Out

I don't care how busy or broke you are, gathering up your peeps and going out for a nice glass of wine, a movie, out dancing, or even having them over for a Saturday morning coffee cake, tea, and chat session is much needed, much deserved, and *dare I say* mandatory for your sanity.

Calendar a movie, dinner, golf, drinks or even a shoe-shopping extravaganza at least once a month.

On the other hand, you might not be up to having that much fun quite yet. I used some of my alone time just to take a nap or read a book. What you're doing isn't as important as the fact that you're actually doing it!

Spirituality

Each person's relationship with his or her creator or higher power is extremely personal, and this section isn't a commercial for any particular belief system. I'm only going to suggest that you have and consistently develop some kind of faith and spiritual practice.

Find books that speak to you, encourage you, and make you think. Find a place of worship where you feel at home. Whatever is resonating with you, making you feel calmer, saner and connected, do more of that.

Tips for Feeling Great

Whether you find the love of your life tomorrow or ten years from now, I want you to look and feel great every single day. Here's a collection of tips to help, and I hope you try the ones that sound great to you, and hopefully they inspire others.

Get fully groomed. Book a mani, pedi, facial, shave, bikini wax, hair cut, color, and highlights, the works. By setting aside time to take care of yourself, you're taking ownership of your self confidence.

Get a crush. Find a brand-new, grown-up crush (hello, George Clooney! Or ... Heidi Klum!). It's great to fantasize. Think of your imagination as your own private playground and feel free to bring whoever you want on "the trip" with you.

Give a gift *to yourself* for no reason. Don't wait for a holiday to give a gift to yourself or to receive a gift from someone. It's not the cost; it's the effort, and we all deserve to give ourselves gifts on a regular basis. Quite possibly you're the only person right now who knows what will make you truly happy.

Try something new. Take a dance class, learn French or Italian, or see an improv comedy show. When you take your life off of auto-pilot, you create new energy and excitement. You might even run into someone special while you're out having a great time.

Dress up. I never loved dressing up until I discovered fashion blogs. Now I love putting together outfits that express my personality. It's fun to play dress up and even more fun to get compliments on how good you'll look. We all have swagger when we know we look great. Get yourself some swagger!

Get your sweat on. Along the lines of trying something new, I took up spinning this year. I love it! I've also discovered there are a lot of great-looking, healthy, and single men in my classes. Why didn't I spin when I was single...? Anyway, the folks are friendly, and when you're new, you can get help adjusting your bike. It's like that anywhere at the gym, and I'm addicted to the endorphins that come with my workouts. You'll be, look, and feel healthier, and what is more attractive than that?

Treat yourself to a massage. I prefer someone coming to my home so I can roll off the table and into the tub or even right into bed. There are lots of cost-effective solutions, including *Massage Envy* to help fulfill your need for touch.

Keep this in mind: when you feel great about you, other people feel great about you! There's no reason *not* do the things that make you feel amazing about yourself. When you can truly love yourself, there will be plenty of space for someone else to love you, too.

There are Plenty of Honest, Fun, and Wonderful People Out There

If while you're reading this chapter, you've found yourself still resistant to the very idea of finding a new special someone, it is probably because you're fairly certain your past partners give you insight into the type of person you'll find when you begin dating. I'm here to tell you *you're going to find exactly whom you are expecting to find.*

There was a time in my coaching business when I was coaching several married men who were either having affairs or flirting with the idea. It seemed everywhere I looked, there were people cheating on their spouses, engaging in deceptive behavior, and acting without integrity. It was awful, and I had no confidence I would find the person who would be faithful! In addition, I'd just broken up with someone who wasn't faithful to me.

Then, I read a book that said "you find exactly what you're looking for based upon what you want to create in your own life." So I decided to do an experiment: I wanted a loving relationship with someone who valued me and would be faithful, so I looked for evidence that those types of relationships existed. Immediately I got an email that one of my girlfriends was celebrating her 12th wedding anniversary and was throwing a dinner party. I'd known my friend and her husband for several years, and they genuinely seemed to love one another. Hmmmm, I thought.

Very shortly thereafter, two separate clients who spoke highly of their wives engaged me during our conversations, and I even met a neighbor who was planning a surprise 50th birthday party for his wife.

Because I defined what I wanted, and looked for evidence it already existed for others, I found it. Then, I found it for myself.

The Art of Dating

Dating after divorce is truly about you and what you want. You may want occasional companionship to get out of the house or office, or you may want to find another spouse and have (more) kids. You are somewhere on the continuum of "I want to see a movie with a fun companion" to "I want to remarry and have kids," and where you are is just fine.

My philosophy on the art of dating is quite simple:

Dating is an opportunity to ask for what you want, say what you're looking for (your purpose for dating), date lots of people (as many as you'd like), have fun and enjoy the process, have almost zero expectation, and remain unattached to the outcome.

When you engage in the art of dating, you actually stand a better chance of ending up with the person who is the best fit for you sooner. Much sooner.

Decide What You Want and Ask for It

There is someone out there who wants for you to give them what you want to give and who will give you what you want to receive.

Author's Note: I suggest you keep repeating this as your mantra until you own it, and it owns you.

Your role in this process is to: decide what you want, then speak your truth (state your dating purpose), sort, continue sorting until you've found the person you're going to date, live with, marry, have children with, all of the above, or none of the above.

Oh yes, and you probably will want to enjoy the process. Therefore, decide right now that you're going to begin this process when, and only when, you can commit to yourself to enjoying the process and not before.

I make it sound so easy, right? Actually it's simple, but I recognize it's not necessarily easy because of the way we are wired and because of the way we're used to doing things.

Here's your new dating process:

1. State your purpose for dating.
2. Have fun and enjoy the process.

3. Have no expectations.
4. Don't be attached to the outcome.

State Your Purpose for Dating

Tell everyone within the sound of your voice what and exactly you're looking to find. They may have a brother, sister, son, daughter, nephew, cousin, co-worker, parent, or neighbor who sounds like a good fit. You just never know where your next Mr., Ms. or Mrs. Wonderful is going to come from. My husband and I met through a mutual friend. His corporate attorney was married to one of my girlfriends. His attorney's wife and I met at a party and became fast friends, and once she realized I was single and asked what I was looking for, I told her. I told lots of other people, too, but she was the one who made the mental connection and the introduction.

If you're so inclined, add yourself to Match.com, eHarmony, OK Cupid, Tinder, and JDate. These services automatically put you in front of people who are also looking, and their profiles explicitly state what they are looking to find. You can voice exactly what you're looking for, and the right person will think that's really great and want to connect with you.

Remember this: you must *a-s-k* to *g-e-t*. All of the wishing and hoping in the world in the comfort of your own home just won't get you the lovin' or love you want. Watching *Grey's Anatomy* will keep you current on the show. Working longer hours will boost your bottom line. Neither of those put you in front of potential love interests! You've got to get busy to get love.

Have Fun and Enjoy the Process

What's the point if you don't have fun and enjoy the process? When all of your energy is wrapped up in "finding," you won't be "enjoying."

I have found, in the process of dating, and even now (still) in the process of building my businesses that staying in a state of curiosity is your best bet for enjoying the process. When I meet new folks, I'm curious about what makes them tick, what they're passionate and excited about, and why they think they're on this planet. Not everyone is a good fit as a friend or client, but everyone has a story, and I want to know it. Make discovering the stories of the people you're dating part of your dating process. Even if the two of you are not a good fit, you could find some really cool, interesting people who might turn out to be great friends.

Inject fun into the dating that you do! Go to new restaurants, indulge in new foods, try miniature golfing, go hiking, learn how to SUP (stand-up paddle), learn a new language, train for a triathlon. All of these activities put you in front of people, many of them new people.

My suggestion is to make a list of restaurants where you want to eat, activities you want to try, and places you want to visit. Then, start doing. Work your way down your list, all the while adding new activities.

I had a blast joining new groups, making new friends, and learning about new things during my single years. An added bonus is that you can make friends with as many people of both sexes as you want. I have many male friends, all of whom I made when I was single.

128

Relationships with the opposite sex are generally not encouraged when you're in a relationship, but if you make them now, the added bonus is not just those relationships, but the fact that those relationships become part of the package that is you.

Have No Expectations

"Is he the one?!" "Is SHE the one?!" "IS THIS THE ONE?!?!" Rinse. Repeat.

I have heard a lot of women and men asking themselves this question very early, even before the first date when they've connected to a "live one."

When you have high expectations that are placed on one potential mate, the chances of those expectations being met are indeed slim. Tonight's could be "the one" (one of many), but chances are they will be another opportunity to refine your desires, get better at dating, have a great time, and meet a cool, new person.

Or, he could be your Mr. Wonderful, and if he could be, and you're in a state of "IS-HE-THE-ONE" panic mode, you'll most likely scare him off. I had more than one guy talk about marriage or the benefits of his job on our first date. Seriously? Too soon everyone!

I know my guy friends, and even my husband, have been bewildered when someone who initially seems pretty great goes too far too fast. If they had just slowed down, it might have worked out.

What if you could just go on a date and the only expectation you have is that you're going to have a conversation (maybe even a good one) and a nice meal? Wouldn't that take the frenetic energy out of the date? The energy that holds **expectation and hope** and even a little bit of crazy? Wouldn't that be nice? Yes, yes it would. Nod and smile, so I know you're with me, okay?

Dating is supposed to be fun. Repeat after me: **Dating is fun.**

Meeting someone new is going to be *fun*. Stating your purpose for dating is going to be *fun*. Eating out is going to be *fun*. Having some grown-up, non-children time is going to be *fun*. The evening out was successful if, at the end of it, you actually want to go on another date!

Do yourself and your sanity a favor and detach yourself from expectations. Before you go on each date, remind yourself that in order to have fun, the best expectation is no expectation. That way, you will be pleasantly surprised when, eventually, something great does happen, and you meet someone with whom you want to spend a measureable amount of time.

Don't Be Attached to the Outcome

My friend, Beth, who introduced me to my husband, tried to get us together for months. I was happily single, working on my businesses, and raising my daughter. I was so unattached to the outcome, that I (incorrectly) predicted the outcome of our first date. I told her to have no expectations because when I "didn't fall in love with him and marry him," I didn't want her to be upset.

I was so not into dating that I went on a date almost against my will. I was completely unattached. I'm sure you've heard the saying, "When you least expect it, expect it." That was me. I didn't expect it, even though I was clear on my purpose for dating; therefore, in a way, I was expecting it, and that's when it happened.

It's up to you to speak your purpose for dating, go on dates, have a great time (even if your date is not having a great time with you), and go on your merry way. If you go on another date, great. If you end up together *forever*, terrific! If you don't, just keep on keepin' on.

Your outcome is your purpose for dating: that's the "Big Outcome" you want to have happen at the right time in the future. In the meantime, you're working, perhaps caring for your kids, making new friends, and creating an incredible future. Right? Right!

Coach's Challenge

Doing all four of these challenges will require courage, for it takes courage to do something new and different in order to get new and different results.

I'm going to challenge you to do just that: something different. Maybe many things different. If you usually go on a date and get into a relationship, try going on a half-dozen dates with the same guy before you commit and take yourself off the market.

If you have had three first dates and three relationships, take the plunge into the deep end of the pool and go on ten first dates. If you think you have to dress a certain way, and that way isn't you in your fullest sense, wear what makes you the most comfortable and attractive *to yourself.* Remember, you're most attractive to others when you're authentically yourself and most attractive to yourself.

Do the thing that scares you the most when it comes to dating. Shake things up. Shake yourself up! You deserve to try something new and get a new, great result.

Sort!

Going on lots of dates is simply "sorting." You're sorting through the possibilities to find someone who is a perfect fit for you. There are so many people, you couldn't possibly date them all before finding a companion who makes you feel amazing.

Perhaps it's a good idea to decide, right now, to date one hundred men in the next year. Too many? Okay, then what's your number? When you have a big enough number, and you keep it in mind, you'll be more apt to remember you're *sorting* and be open to trying out lots of different potential mates before settling on one.

Speak Your Truth

When you are dating, you have the perfect opportunities to speak your truth: you're a single parent, you're excited about your career (or the new business you want to start), and you're dating because ... insert "your purpose for dating here."

This may mean that if it's cold outside, and you want to wear jeans and boots and a heavy coat instead of a short skirt and heels, do that. Just double-check with your date that he doesn't have a "short skirt, heels, and fancy dress" date planned.

132

That's what I did. It was December and unseasonably cold outside when my husband and I were planning our first date. While the girl in me wanted to wear a silk blouse, a skirt, high heels, and a fun, light jacket, I knew I would be miserable and counting the moments until I could get in my car and crank up the heat. Not necessarily the best plan for having an enjoyable evening.

So, when my now-husband asked about meeting at a particular outdoor location and walking around, I said, "Since it's on the chilly side, are you okay if I wear jeans and boots so I don't freeze to death?" Wouldn't you know, he was perfectly fine with me wearing whatever I wanted. In fact, that's what he wore, too.

Pretty soon, I'll address why speaking your truth is so important.

As your coach, at least for the duration of this book, I want you to start speaking your truth at every turn, in every situation, and to everyone. All the time, no matter what. Start building that muscle by asking for what you want all the time. If you want to go to a different restaurant, suggest it. If you want more salary, ask for it. If you're uncomfortable in a situation, let those around you know. Getting stronger in any area of your life starts with taking action in the direction you want to go. Speaking your truth will make your life better in all areas, not just in love.

Try it. You'll like it. (I promise.)

Save Yourself for the Best Fit (a.k.a. You Deserve the Best!)

This part is where I insist you not settle. Good enough is just not good enough.

This process isn't about finding Mr. Perfect. He just simply doesn't exist. This process is about finding Mr. Perfect-For-You. My husband isn't perfect (pretty darn close), but he is perfect for me. We compliment each other so well, and that makes our relationship harmonious -- most days, anyway. I'm so clear I'm not perfect, but he swears I'm perfect for him. That's a pretty great feeling: a feeling you, too, deserve to have.

I always say it's better to be single and happy than to be in a relationship and miserable. If you're divorced, I'm sure right about now you're nodding your head. Don't settle, and you won't end up divorced or on the other side of a broken relationship again wishing you hadn't.

Sex After Divorce

You might be thinking, *"What are you, crazy?"* After a divorce, the thought of dating again and having a sexual relationship with someone new can be scary and difficult. I know it was for me. As a matter of fact, when someone suggested it, I broke down in tears!

For some people, it's like being in high school, starting all over again. But while you may be swept away by a new romance, there are some down-to-earth issues to grapple with.

134

How do you introduce your children to a new person? And how do you deal with the issue of safe sex, when both you and the person you are seeing have just gotten out of a marriage?

The rules may have changed since your last dating experience, especially if you're coming out of a longer marriage.

For instance, those who married in their early 20s, and are now in their late 30s and early 40s, did not become sexual in the AIDS era, so they may have some new skills and vocabulary to learn.

Sex is a risk, and it is important to feel safe with the person you're with, to feel a degree of intimacy. If there is any doubt, don't do it.

The Emotional Roller Coaster

Experts say that the prospect of new sexual relationships bring emotions related to your break up to the forefront. Unresolved hurt or anger can affect your sexuality and your ability to get involved in a fulfilling relationship.

If you are not far enough along in the healing process, post-divorce sex can actually make you feel worse, not better. On the other hand, if you are further along on the healing curve, it can be a loving and satisfying experience. Generally, therapists say it takes about two years to heal after a divorce, and to be ready for a relationship again.

Some women avoid sexual contact since rejection has a negative impact on their self-image. If they have been dumped by their spouse, there can be feelings of low self-esteem, or personal failure and abandonment. This can impact how you feel about your sexual attractiveness, and the way you interact with people of the opposite sex.

I recommend setting goals to help define the new you, such as "I want to go on a dinner date this month," or "I will focus on meditating every day for 30 days." Another way to get out of the slump is exercise, such as a brisk, 45-minute walk, to chase away depression and help you feel emotionally grounded.

Wear clothes that give you a lift, perhaps something with a bright color, and by all means dwell on the positive aspects of being single. There are many, some as simple as you get to decide what's for dinner every night, where you vacation, what you're spending money on, and when you go to bed and wake up every day.

Getting Back into a Relationship

Divorce may prompt you to feel like jumping into a sexual relationship right away to regain a sense of power. Let me warn you that jumping in too soon may provide temporary fulfillment, but could lead to hating yourself the next morning.

Wearing condoms may not have been an issue in your marriage, but upon re-entering the dating game, you need to know about and protect yourself from the dangers of unprotected sex.

You can't tell whether someone has a sexually transmitted disease by just looking at them, so remember to practice safe sex. Whatever you do, there should be a good feeling, and a sense of rightness in a new relationship.

Ideally you should talk about it ahead of time, *before* you are in the bedroom. If you can't talk about sex with the person you're about to have sex with, that is probably a sign you shouldn't have sex. Don't you agree?

Moving On:
Your Action Steps for Moving Forward

*Get yourself ready when it's time to be ready: forgive yourself and your ex, fall in love with you, and take excellent care of yourself.
*Put on a rock-star attitude!
*Master the art of dating, including defining your Purpose for Dating.
*Have FUN. Go on GNOs: girls' and guys' nights out. You deserve them; do them!
*Remember: you deserve the very best!

"If you can't remember the last time you had fun, pull out your phone and schedule something right now!"
~Honorée Corder

Chapter Nine:
Bonus: If Co-Parenting is a Game, These are the Rules!

"Your divorce is about you, not your kids. Make sure they know that, too." ~Honorée Corder

If you had children during your marriage, you are inextricably linked to your ex until … well, forever. That means you can't cut off *all* communication and get on with your life. You have to find a way to help your children understand their new life even as you're getting a handle on yours. You'll have to find a way to communicate with someone you may not have had a good conversation with in years. And, you *must* do it because your kids and their mental health depends on it.

Right now, your kids are probably scared and unsure of their future. Divorce, even on the friendliest of terms, is not an ideal situation for adults. For children, it is downright frightening.

They don't have a clue what is truly happening and are attempting to understand an almost incomprehensible situation. I know, kind of like what's going on with you right now.

Put yourself in their shoes, just for a moment. How do you feel when you don't know what's happening? Immediately you feel stressed and anxious. It's like driving in the middle of the night, going 80 mph, with no lights on. You might just crash into something at any moment, and you'd probably be freaking out. Yup, that's how your 11-year-old feels right about now.

Kids may not know everything that's happening, but there's no doubt about it: kids can feel something is wrong and it can take them off their center, making them feel insecure and unsure.

At any age, your kids will feel uncertain, sad, or angry at the prospect of mom and dad splitting up.

Rule #1: Deal with Your Divorce Like a Grownup ... for the Kids

Your kids *know* what's up. They know things are different, what's going on feels wrong, even if they aren't old enough to know exactly what different or wrong means.

As a parent, you absolutely can make the divorce process less painful for your children. Helping your kids cope with divorce means providing stability in your home and tending to their needs with a reassuring, positive attitude. It won't be a seamless process, but there are several things you and your ex can do that can help them cope.

During any phase of the divorce process, it is normal to feel uncertain about how to give your children the right support. It may be uncharted territory, but you *can* successfully navigate this unsettling time, and help your kids emerge from it feeling loved, confident, and strong. Your patience, reassurance, and listening ear can minimize tension as children learn to cope with new circumstances. By providing routines kids can rely on and taking the time to ask questions and really listen, you remind children they can count on you for stability, structure, and care. And, if (when!) you can maintain a positive co-parenting relationship with your ex, you can help kids avoid the stress and fear that comes from watching parents in conflict. Such a transitional time can't be without some measure of hardship, but you can powerfully reduce your children's pain by making their well-being one of your top priorities.

This letter should help you understand what your kids need as you help them move through your divorce into their new life:

A Letter from a Child of Divorce

Dear Mom and Dad,

I realize something is happening, but I don't really know what it is. Life is different, I'm scared to death and unsure of my future. Here's what I need from you, my parents:

I need both of you to stay involved in my life. When I'm not with you, please write letters, make phone calls, and ask me lots of questions. When you don't stay involved and I don't hear from you, I feel like I'm not important and that you don't really love me.

I need to see you. Make time for me, no matter how far apart we are, or how busy or poor you are. I miss you when we're not together. When you're out of sight, I think you've forgotten me and don't love me.

I need you to please stop fighting and work hard to get along with each other. Figure out how to agree on matters related to me. When you fight about me, I think that I did something wrong, and I feel guilty.

I need to feel like it is okay to love you both. I need to feel like it is okay to enjoy the time that I spend with each of you. Please support me and the time that I spend with each of you. If you act jealous or upset, I feel like I need to take sides and love one parent more than the other.

I need you to find a way to positively and directly communicate with each other about me, and everything I need or want. Please don't put me in the middle or make me the messenger.

I need you to say only nice things about each other, because I am half of both of you and I love both of you equally. When you say mean, unkind things about my other parent, I feel like you don't like them, and therefore, you don't like me. I also feel like you are putting me in the middle and asking me to choose one of you over the other.

I need both of my parents. Please remember that I want both of you to be a part of my life. I count on my mom and dad to raise me, to teach me what is important, and to help me when I have problems.

Thank you.

Love, Your Child

Rule #2: The Divorce is Not their Fault, But They Will Think It Is

Your divorce is the result of a relationship that didn't work out. You couldn't get along, someone couldn't keep their pants on, there is drug and alcohol abuse, or worse. Except under the most extreme of circumstances, I think we can all agree that the cause of your divorce isn't your children. But that doesn't mean that little Johnny doesn't hold himself responsible for your fighting, wish you could just get along, and cry himself to sleep every night while hoping his family would stay happily together.

Children tend to be egocentric and blame themselves for their parents' divorce. In addition, they may feel it is their responsibility to bring the parents back together. You know your kids aren't to blame, but they don't know that ... unless and until they hear it enough times from you.

Prior to separating, it is important to discuss the impending divorce in age-appropriate terms. Reassure your kids the divorce is *not* their fault, both parents love them very much, and you are there to listen and answer any questions they have. Get everyone possible in on this conversation: your parents, your ex's parents, aunts, uncles, and close friends. You never know which person is going to say the right thing at the right time, and help your kids to shift into feeling like everything is still going to turn out okay.

My daughter *still* has questions, more than a decade after my divorce. The older she gets, and the deeper her understanding, the more she wants to know about my relationship with her dad, what went wrong, and most recently, am I still glad I had a child? More on that soon.

Rule #3: The Kids Need Help, Too

As we discussed in Chapter Two, putting a strong team around you helps you survive and thrive through the divorce process. Your kids can benefit from having a strong team surrounding them, too.

Their team will consist of their parents, of course, other relatives, some friends, and in my opinion, a therapist. If your therapist has experience working with children, allow your child to visit with them alone. Or, seek out a family systems specialist or someone specializing in child therapy, specifically children of divorce.

About the time my daughter entered kindergarten, she started to act out on an almost daily basis. I believe it was because she saw other dads show up for them in a variety of ways (attending school activities, playing with them at the park, etc.) and her friends all had still-married parents at that time. She noticed she didn't have the same thing, and started to be angry and frustrated about it. At such a young age, she wasn't equipped to know what to do with those emotions. How that manifested was that she wouldn't stay with anyone who wasn't me unless she was attending school. Babysitters ran screaming from our home, and if I had something I had to do, she threw such incredible temper tantrums that I was called and requested home immediately. And, to make it even more fun, she was throwing extra large tantrums just for me.

Because I was at a loss of what to do, and up against my own parenting limitations, when one of my clients recommended a therapist, I called immediately and left a message. When the therapist called back, I was full of emotion because I literally felt like help was on the line and, well, I needed help. I just didn't know what exactly to do to help my daughter, and felt at a loss for what to do next.

The therapist laid out a clear set of rules: whatever was said in therapy was confidential, and I was not to ask questions of my daughter after the session. Therapy was meant to be my daughter's safe place to discuss what was on her mind, and that's exactly what happened. It also became a safe place for me to learn tools that I lacked. We learn how to parent from modeling our parents, after all. I didn't want what I had seen in my childhood to become how I parented. Over time, the therapist gave us both tools for dealing with each other, all the while providing advice, tips, strategies and of course, calling us out when necessary. When I was being cranky or unreasonable, I heard about it. When my daughter was being overly dramatic, she heard about it. We learned a lot about what healthy and normal was like.

Best of all, when a situation came up (I wanted to introduce my now-husband to my daughter; she wasn't making friends easily in school), we had an unbiased, neutral third-party trained in how to help us deal effectively with them.

If you are now a divorced parent without a solid set of parenting tools, I recommend therapy as a possible solution for your kids. If your child feels sad, confused, angry, resentful, or frustrated about the divorce, therapy really could be helpful and not just for your kids. Your kids engaging in an effective therapeutic relationship could be helpful for all of you.

If your kids are asking questions you don't know how to answer, a therapist can bridge that gap. They can also provide a soft place to fall, a safe place, to process what's happening and get a handle on it.

Get your kids the help they need and be confident about it. Only you can decide what might help your kids, and they are relying on you to do the right thing for them.

There are normal reactions to separation and divorce, and there are signs your kids may be affected more deeply than you are equipped to handle.

Although strong feelings can be tough on kids, the following reactions can be considered normal for children.

- **Anger.** Your kids may express their anger, rage, and resentment with you and your ex for destroying their sense of normalcy.
- **Anxiety.** It's natural for children to feel anxious when faced with big changes in their lives.
- **Mild depression.** Sadness about the family's new situation is normal, and sadness coupled with a sense of hopelessness and helplessness is likely to become a mild form of depression.

It will take some time for your kids to work through their issues about the separation or divorce, but you should see gradual improvement over time.

Red Flags

If your child's behaviors get worse rather than better after several months, it may be a sign that your child is stuck in depression, anxiety, or anger and could use some additional support. Watch for these warning signs of divorce-related depression or anxiety:

- Sleep problems
- Poor concentration
- Trouble at school
- Drug or alcohol abuse
- Self-injury, cutting, or eating disorders
- Frequent angry or violent outbursts
- Withdrawal from loved ones
- Refusal of loved activities

There's no need to panic, but you will want to immediately discuss these or other divorce-related warning signs with your child's other parent, doctor, and teachers, and consult a child therapist for guidance on coping with specific problems.

Rule #4: Clear, Healthy Communication {i.e., NO Fighting In Front Of, or Near Your Kids, or Where They Could Overhear You

The things that really pissed you off about your spouse while you were married are still going to upset you, probably more so now that you're divorced. If he never really heard you when you were married, you can bet he's not more open to listening to you now. If she was a hot, disorganized mess when you were happily coupled up, chances are she's even more so today. But guess what, sunshine? None of that matters today. What does matter today is that you put the past where it belongs: in the past, and figure out a way to communicate that gives your children peace of mind.

The best thing happily married parents can do to provide their kids with a healthy home environment is have loving, clear communication. This demonstrates to them they are safe and loved and can go about the business of growing up.

It stands to reason that the best thing divorced parents can do to provide their kids with a healthy home environment is have loving, clear communication. You can roll your eyes at me all you want (yes, I saw that). I'm here to acknowledge that you may not love your ex anymore, but you do love your little pumpkins and for sure you don't want to do anything to hurt them. RIGHT? Right.

So what you're going to do is be respectful and nice every single time you see your ex or talk to him on the phone *when your children might possibly hear you.* You are probably going to have words on occasion with your ex. After all, if you could communicate brilliantly, you might possibly still be brilliantly married. You will, from time to time, need to hash out a thing or two. Do it while your kids are nowhere around. If your kids are home, take a drive without them. If you try to resolve something and your kids can hear one or both sides of the conversation, table the conversation until later (such as when they are at school) or physically take yourself to another location.

I tried to listen to everything my parents talked about when I was a kid, and your kids are just as curious about what you're up to. My daughter gets caught all the time standing outside of my office and bedroom doors trying to overhear what my husband and I are discussing. Humans are naturally curious creatures, and your kids are no exception.

148

If your conversations are still a bit frosty, keep them brief and outcome focused. Be as nice as you possibly can, then say good-bye and get on with your day. Why? Because, you are getting along with your ex for your kids, not for you or your ex.

Rule #5: Always Speak About Your Kid's Other Parent POSITIVELY

Your kids don't know every reason you are getting a divorce. You shouldn't tell them everything, so of course they don't know everything. If you've discovered your ex is a madam parading around as a soccer mom, it might be tempting to let little Johnny in on the secret in an attempt to get him to take your side and turn against his mom. Not your best idea.

If your ex has moved in with his 22-year-old secretary, it is almost an irresistible situation to share with your sister, mom, *and* teenaged daughter.

Your kids are not your friends, they are your children. Children need to be in the dark about the adult goings-on of their parents. Especially when said goings-on are actions that could cause their relationship with that parent to diminish or be disrupted completely. We are all human, and all humans make mistakes. Our children shouldn't really be privy to just how human we are, or our mistakes, at least not until they are old enough to truly understand them. If your kids are still kids, i.e., under the age of let's say 25, keep them in the dark.

Haven't we addressed how to act around your kids with regards to your ex multiple times in multiple ways? Yep. Did you read it *and* internalize it? Have you stopped rolling your eyes when your ex calls to talk to your kids? Do you still change the tone of your voice when referring to *"her"* or are you still peeved at your ex and your kids know all about it? Have you connected the dots about how your behavior can undermine your kids' well-being and cause them to question their love, safety, and general well-being?

If you haven't, then listen up! I'm not a sugar-coater. I'm about as direct as they come, and I'm about to take it up a notch.

Your kids are half of their other parent, so when you say something negative about your kids' mom or dad, they believe you think they are half-bad as well.

Stop doing this immediately.

In fact, you need to connect with your ex's great qualities and characteristics *and regularly share them with your kids.*

Examples: *"One of the things I love about your dad is how great he is at his job." "Your mom has always been the best cook I know." "Your father is a top-notch [insert profession or hobby] and you should ask him about it sometime."*

You validate your kids when you validate their other parent. Don't try to think of a way to talk about how much of a world-class sneak they are, you're going to make a list of genuine, bona-fide positive qualities and characteristics about your ex. And, you're going to talk about them with your kids. It will give them a strong sense of security during a time when they are definitely not feeling all that secure.

Got it? Good.

150

Rule #6: Co-Parent like Champions

I'm going to make some broad assumptions here: that your ex isn't a true danger mentally, physically, or emotionally to your kids. This advice isn't necessarily for a divorced person whose spouse is an alcoholic, has a crazy drug-addiction, or is violent. If this is you, please seek the help of a great therapist and family law attorney.

If, on the other hand and as we've discussed, you're just pretty pissed off at your ex because he cheated on you, never held down a job (or worked 24/7), and/or was a narcissist, you've got to do what's right for your kids: get over it, and get on with it.

Here are some suggestions for co-parenting effectively:

- Hammer out a visitation schedule that works as well as possible for everyone. Do your best to stick to that schedule, and be willing to be flexible when necessary.

- Keep your ex in the loop about grades and school, friends, and health issues. Especially if your ex lives far away, sending a text or email every so often about what's happening will help calm the waters. Also, it's helpful to have an ex you can call when your kids need cash contributions for the inevitable expenses that pop up, such as school pictures, yearbooks, field trips, and extracurricular activities, when the kids are sick, or you have to work late and need an extra set of hands. You get more flies with honey than vinegar, and again, your kids need for you to win that Oscar for nice behavior if you have to!

- Respect your ex's parenting boundaries and behavioral guidelines. You and your ex may disagree about bedtimes, what's appropriate television, even the right diet for your kids. But what goes on at your ex's house, as long as it doesn't endanger your kids, needs to be respected. If your kids complain, remind them they need to respect the rules at each parent's house.

- Agree with your ex that you absolutely won't disparage each other to your children, and absolutely forbid your children to speak disrespectfully about the other parent, even though it may be music to your ears.

- Be nice. Once your ex realizes you're on the "up-and-up" (and not trying to pull a fast one, lie or hide anything) you can have a pretty good relationship with open communication.

- Know that your kids will test boundaries and try to pit one parent against the other. Never make assumptions about the other parent without talking with her first. Commit to having regular conversations about the kids so they know they can't manipulate you.

If your ex is particularly difficult, think of being a co-parenting rock star this way: you will set one heck of a great example for your kids about how to deal with difficult people. Let's face it, your kids are going to meet some pretty ugly people in their lifetime and they need skills -- the same skills you're going to develop, finely tune, and model for them will come in handy more than once (a week) starting in about the third grade.

I'm not saying it's going to be easy. I'm saying it's completely necessary. You owe it to yourself, your peace of mind, and your kids.

"Once you get past the grief, magical things can happen if you are open to them. My alcoholic jerk of an ex became the supportive dad who really stepped up when my daughter needed him. I would never have predicted that! Miracles can happen!" ~Alissa McAffee

Rule #7: Be Mindful of New Relationships and How They Affect Your Children, and Your Ex

After a divorce, children often wish their parents would get back together, and it is difficult to introduce anyone new to them you may be dating. Just as you have had to grapple with the fact that your marriage ended, so, too will your children. And, it will take possibly longer or be harder for them to process and understand.

It is generally accepted that you should not bring anyone into the children's lives unless it is someone with whom you have a firm commitment. If the child becomes attached to the person, it would be difficult for him or her to suffer yet another loss in their lives.

You may be so excited about your new love interest, but your ex is another story. They may be thrilled to get you out of their hair and delighted you've moved on. Or, they may still be swirling in hurt and devastation and the fact that you're dating could be salt in their wound.

Do not let your children or your ex decide whether you see someone or not, but respect their feelings. They may feel frightened or angry at the prospect of you having a new mate, but allow them to talk about these feelings.

If you get to the point where you are going to remarry, waiting to do so allows children the chance to get used to it. Children should understand that it is okay to like the new person, even if they are still harboring negative feelings about the divorce. Additionally, be sure to keep your ex in the loop as they shouldn't find out from anyone other than you that you are permanently adding a new person to their children's lives.

The Kids

What is the best time to introduce a new partner to your children? Chances are we've all heard stories about someone who introduced their kids too soon, and it ruined the relationship or caused a huge rift between them and their kids. I think we can all agree that dating after divorce when you have kids can be tricky. The number one thing to keep in mind is not to do it too soon after your divorce, or even while you're still in the process of the divorce. After all, what's the hurry?

Even if both of you are in love and seem to have a lot in common, breakups during these first two critical years after divorce (not to mention relationships that begin before a divorce is final) are common and kids get caught in the crossfire. Next, the setting and timing of an introduction is crucial to success. Rather than planning an overnight or long visit, plan to have a brief, casual meeting with few expectations.

Keep in mind the age of your children when introducing them to a new love interest, because younger children (under age 10) may feel confused, angry, or sad since they tend to be possessive of their parents. Renowned researcher Constance Ahrons, who conducted a twenty-year study of children of divorce, determined that most children find their parent's courtship behaviors confusing and strange. Your older child may seem more accepting and appear to be able to tolerate your new partner better. However, they may feel threatened by this relationship. Ahrons also found that teenagers can find open affection between their parent and a partner troubling. Keep your distance and go easy on physical contact with your new paramour in front of your kids.

Consider that you are a role model for your children. Exposing them to casual partners does not set the best example for responsible dating. Our children, especially our teenage children, tend to model their behavior after us. Keeping the best interests of your children in mind will help you to make wise decisions about dating after your divorce. You owe it to yourself and your kids to build new relationships thoughtfully.

Five Tips for introducing your new partner to your kids:

- Talk to your children and explain that you are dating someone whom you care about and that you'd like to introduce them in the near future. Be sure to ask them if they have any

155

questions, validate their concerns, and most of all, *listen.*

- Keep the first meeting short and low key. Going to a restaurant or neutral spot is best. Ask your kids where they'd like to go, and don't invite your partner's children to join you on the first few visits.

- Don't plan an overnight or long weekend right away. If you have shared custody, it should be easy to spend an overnight with your new love when your children are with your ex. Having your new partner spend the night should only be an option once you are fairly sure that your relationship is permanent or you are engaged.

- Assure your kids that your partner will not replace their other parent or change your relationship with them. Again, most young children view their parent's dating behaviors as confusing. If they are especially close to their other parent or they have had you all to themselves for a while, they may feel threatened or resentful about having to share you with another person.

- Have realistic expectations about your children's acceptance of your new partner. Just because you are enthralled with this person, they may not share your enthusiasm.

Being cautious while dating after divorce when you have kids will pay off for everyone. Consider the amount of time since your divorce, the age of your children, and the level of commitment with your partner. Don't introduce your children to new partners whom you are dating casually. You can inform your kids that you are going out with friends and that's enough information.

Talking through your plans with your coach or therapist may help you to make a smooth transition into this next phase of your life.

The Ex

When you find a person with whom you are having a significant relationship, tell your ex. I'm not talking about casual dating or the fun you're having on the weekends while the kids are with their other parent. Neither your kids nor your ex need to know anything about what you're doing during your free time.

But a new committed partner, whether she is going to be your new spouse or not, is a new person in your children's lives – and the other parent needs to be kept in the loop. While she doesn't need or want to know everything, she has a right to know who her children are spending a measurable amount of time with and feel at least reasonably comfortable about it.

What Your Kids Need Most: The Reassurance and Love of Both Parents

Children have a remarkable ability to heal when given the support and love they need. Your words, actions, and ability to remain consistent are all important tools to reassure your children of your unchanging love.

- **Both parents will be there.** Let your kids know that even though the physical circumstances of the family unit will change, they can continue to have healthy,

157

loving relationships with both of their parents.

- **It'll be okay.** Tell kids that things won't always be easy, but that they will work out. Knowing it'll be all right can provide incentive for your kids to give a new situation a chance.
- **Closeness.** Physical closeness, in the form of hugs, pats on the shoulder, or simple proximity, has a powerful way of reassuring your child of your love.
- **Be honest.** When kids raise concerns or anxieties, respond truthfully. If you don't know the answer, say gently that you aren't sure right now, but you'll find out and it will be okay.

Providing stability and structure

While it's good for kids to learn to be flexible, adjusting to many new things at once can be very difficult. Help your kids adjust to change by providing as much stability and structure as possible in their daily lives.

Remember that establishing structure and continuity doesn't mean that you need rigid schedules or that mom and dad's routines need to be exactly the same. But creating some regular routines at each household and consistently communicating to your children what to expect will provide your kids with a sense of calm and stability.

*"You CAN co-parent with a smile, your way.
Do it and your kids will thank you for it!"*
~Honorée Corder

Chapter Ten:
Your Divorce is Not the End, It is Your New Beginning

"Divorce is your new beginning. I hope you're full of positive anticipation, because you're going to love what happens next."
~Honorée Corder

I started this book by saying divorce was not just an end, it was also a beginning. If someone had told me that a dozen years post-divorce I would be happily remarried, in a career I love, and have a lovely 14-year-old daughter, I would have thought they were genuinely crazy.

I didn't "luck" into a happier life after divorce. Getting to a place in my life where I'm genuinely happy, *most of the time*, in every area, wasn't an accident. I intentionally decided to turn my divorce lemons into a lifetime of yummy lemonade. But I didn't realize I had the power to decide as early as I could have. No one told me my divorce was a blessing in disguise, and I certainly didn't feel like it was for a long time!

One of the reasons I wrote this book was to empower you to look at your divorce with rose-tinted glasses until your official rose-colored glasses arrive! You absolutely can create a life where you wake up every day thrilled to be alive.

In case you don't believe me, keep reading!

159

What Divorced People Say

"Let the past stay in the past. Learn your lessons from it and move on. Live in today and look forward to the future. Better things are coming your way!"
~Donna Johnson Magers

"When going through divorce, don't lose the plot. Sometimes it makes sense to stop fighting before you're ready, settle and allow the whole family to move on."
~Emma Johnson

"It's hard to get anywhere walking backwards; let the past go, turn and look forward, because tomorrow is fresh and new and ready for you to make your own."
~Morghan Martell Richardson

"My whole world turned upside down ...
and I kinda like it!!!"
~Clarissa Ramirez Norcross

"No matter what the circumstances, it is a choice to be a victim or a victor. So, be kind to yourself, allow yourself time to process what has happened, learn from it, and move toward your highest joy. So many folks shut down after divorce. It took me years to create a space in my heart, to open up and be vulnerable again. No voids go unfilled IN THE UNIVERSE. You must create the space for someone wonderful to come in, then, it can happen. ~Dan Malin

"It's been eight years this month since the night I learned that my first wife decided to move on. It's been three years this month since I remarried. Those five years in between were some of the hardest of my life, but I can honestly say, I'm the happiest I've ever been. If I could have talked to myself eight years ago I would have said, "The best is yet to come. Don't believe me? Just try and prove me wrong.!"
~Joey McGirr

What's in Store for You

Freedom

One of the benefits of getting a divorce is new found freedom. Those getting a divorce are no longer questioned regarding their every move and every decision. They have no one to account to other than themselves. A great weight is lifted and life will eventually present many new and exciting opportunities.

You now have the freedom to discover yourself in ways that may have been impossible during your marriage. You can travel, learn new languages, change careers, and yes, find new love. In fact, being single gives you the freedom to discover not only how interesting you are, but how interesting many of the other occupants of the planet are as well. There are lots of resources on dating after divorce, so all I'll say here is there are a lot of supremely interesting people you can get to know now that would have frankly been inappropriate while you were still married.

Happiness

Getting a divorce will not magically make life perfect, but as the source of the negativity in your old life departs, a great weight is lifted. Your new-found happiness is one of the best benefits of getting a divorce. Life is too short to live with turmoil, stress, or suffering, and you can now be "you" again after perhaps many years of trying to become who someone else wanted you to be.

Just Keep Putting One Foot In Front of the Other

Divorce might feel like the end of the world at first, but eventually everything works out for the best. This isn't speculation, my friend, this is reassurance you can bank on. If you are still overwhelmed with the complexity and emotions of your divorce, your only job right now is to continue to put one foot in front of the other. You won't jump from all-consuming sadness to relief and joy overnight. But little by little, day-by-day, you will work through the process and begin to feel better, and then much better, and then all better.

You've Got This!

You may not think you're making progress. You may wonder why today was worse than yesterday, and why it feels like you take a few steps forward and many steps back. I read something profound recently:

> *You have an undefeated record of surviving bad days.*

This time in your life, your divorce, is no different really, than many of the other bad days you've weathered in your life.

What's Next ...

You've read this far and regardless of where you are in the divorce process, you're one step and one day closer to your new life. Your best chances for success lie in you getting through your divorce by following the suggestions in this book, those given to you by your attorney, your therapist, and your coach.

You can do it, so do it!

> *"The best days of your life start today."*
> ~Honorée Corder

Divorce Transformation Coaching Program™ (DTCP™) Options

The Divorce Transformation Coaching Program™ Overview

In this program, you will receive one-on-one focus, attention, and accountability from a certified DTCP™ coach who has been through a divorce and knows how to help you navigate the challenges and emotions, while facilitating your amazing transformation.

When you are ready to jump-start your new life, heal from your separation and divorce, and take it to a whole new level, we are ready for you. Every divorcing and divorced person faces the challenge of healing and moving forward, adjusting to single life, keeping the house in order, being supportive to his or her children, practicing excellent self-care, perhaps balancing personal and professional life -- and there are, of course, many others.

The **Divorce Transformation Coaching Program™ (DTCP™)** was designed especially to help you get your life back, and your game on, after divorce. Contact Honorée Enterprises COO Joan Richardson at Joan@CoachHonoree.com or 214-422-3965 to be connected with a DTCP™ coach perfect for you.

<u>Gratitude</u>

My life works because the best people surround me. This book was written because I had the love and support of some pretty crazy-amazing people!

To my husband, partner, and best friend, Byron. It's awesome being married to the coolest person I know. I love you.

To my daughter and inspiration, Lexi, I'm so grateful to be your mom. Thank you for being so awesome! I love you.

To my bestie, back-up singer, and shoe-shopping partner, Joan, you're just the greatest. I love having you to work with, play with, and shop with.

To my mastermind peeps, Rich, Andrea, Scott, and Jerald ~ I'm so grateful for your support, ideas, and our synergy.

Who is Honorée

Honorée Corder became an instant single mom when she divorced in 2004. She has gone on to turn her divorce into one of the best things ever to happen to her. She is the best-selling author of a dozen books, including *Vision to Reality*, *The Successful Single Mom* book series, *The Successful Single Dad*, *Play2Pay*, *Paying4College*, and *Tall Order!* She is also an entrepreneur, keynote speaker, and executive coach. She empowers others to dream big and go for what they truly want before, during, and after divorce.

Her ground-breaking coaching programs provide support for those navigating divorce. The Divorce Transformation Coaching Program is currently available for individuals going through or who have gone through a divorce.

Honorée Enterprises, Inc.
Honoree@CoachHonoree.com
http://www.HonoreeCorder.com
Twitter: @Honoree & @Singlemombooks
Facebook: http://www.facebook.com/Honoree

39437598R00098

Made in the USA
San Bernardino, CA
20 June 2019